ON IT

Jonathan Robinson

ISBN 978-1503001800

Cover design by Vadoo Ltd and the author.

All photographs in this book are by the author.

Back cover photograph by Alex Fine.

www.jonathanrobinson.org

For you know who

Introduction

By Jonathan Aitken

Jonathan Robinson is a prison reform campaigner who never takes 'no' for an answer. His honest and hilarious first book *IN IT* – the warts and all diary he penned during his sentence – ruffled many feathers in the HMPS aviary.

Now his sequel *ON IT* turns the author's guns towards the failure of most prison establishments to take rehabilitation seriously.

I say "failure" but *ON IT* reports one outstanding rehabilitation success story. This is the account of Robinson's personal triumph in persuading the Ministry of Justice to make *Toe by Toe* (a proven prisoner to prisoner literary programme) universally available in all jails.

How Jonathan Robinson thumped so persistently on the doors of the great, the good and the grey of the prison bureaucracy when fighting to win support for his crusade is a cautionary tale of our times. Readers of *ON IT* may well be shocked, surprised, and in some cases deeply disappointed by the apathy and obstructionism Robinson encountered. I certainly was.

But few will be disappointed by *ON IT*. This is a thumping good read.

Jonathan Aitken

31 January 2014.

ON IT

When I sit down to write a book, I do not say to myself, 'I am going to produce a work of art.' I write it because there is some lie that I want to expose, some fact to which I want to draw attention, and my initial concern is to get a hearing.

George Orwell

ON IT

Are you sitting comfortably? Then I'll begin…

Actually I'll stop right there. If you're reading this and have not read IN IT can I please urge you to rapidly close this up and peruse the last volume of my penned-prattling. This is *not* some ghastly estate-agent sales spiel that a property backing on to the district line's tracks is in the green-belt, rather an explanation that if you attempt digestion of the following without being au fait with previous events then what lies before you will make little sense – a bit like the way our prisons are run… A desire to scale the north face of ON IT without previously reaching the vertiginous summit of IN IT would be like reading an Agatha Christie book backwards. Trust me – I'm an ex-prisoner, innit.

Right, now that's sorted. Off we go.

During my flying days a very diverse gathering of people came and went through the mechanisms of committing aviation involving this individual. A diversity as wide as that found within our country's prison population as a point of fact. You name it, the spectrum who bounced to the blue-yonder and back spreads from film stars to brickies.

One was a Bishop.

I suppose I should have cottoned-on that this high ranking member of the God-squad was not your average mitre master by his rather unorthodox method of transport. He arrived on the most enormous motorcycle that had more chrome wrapped around it than Detroit used to turn out during the heyday of its automobile business. His apparel was rather catching too. Black leather was in abundance. Everywhere. Suzi Quatro quotas. With tassels.

Once airborne I voiced my normal question of ensuring my passenger's comfort and posed the query if he was enjoying the flight. His response was non-standard Vatican phraseology.

"Fucking great!"

This more than tickled me. Chuckling, I probed further and asked if our closer proximity to his boss had been noted by him. Swiss Guards who patrol Papal premises would I imagine have flinched somewhat with the flying Bishop's response.

"Fucking right! Let's hope we don't fucking meet him!"

Quite how I continued the flight without breaking out in hysterics I will never know.

Certain conclusion that I was surely about to meet my maker on being told I was off to *Shawshank* land has been previously documented. This collection of words is what happened (to this idiot) post clink. The melting pot includes trying to get something done about the so called 'rehabilitation' allegedly taking place inside the parlous state of prison which has involved rather a lot of Vaquero cattle driving door-beating. I have thrown in various other skirmishes that have taken place during the navigation of this rocky road.

If I can say right now that what totally knocked me for six during my incarceration was firstly the astonishing untapped potential of some of my fellows and secondly the demoniac lack of passion and innovation in the lugubrious languid establishments that pen them. One and all demonstrate agreement that prison doesn't work. By all means punish offenders who get sent there – but a new very large clean sheet of paper needs to be unfurled on the modal of what to do with them whilst they are guests of Her Majesty, for the existing tumbleweed in-prison rehabilitation innovation currently blowing by is nothing more than a mild breeze that would struggle to make a curtain swirl. It barely tips its hat at the derelict debris.

My return to earth from prison has been different – I suspect – to others' as not all spend their time trying to make some sense of 320,000 muckraking words written during their sentence, then edit them – and then set out on the warpath to promote the end product – in attempt to raise awareness of my primary focus, which has been and always will be the unimpeachable verging on criminal levels of illiteracy in our prisons and more vitally, the unfathomable barring (you read that right) of the common-sense in-house remedy of this curable cancer. If somehow IN IT transmuted a declaration of war on this front when it broke surface – stirred the tanks – I am more than happy.

When James Garner asks Donald Pleasance in *that* film "What are you *doing* here?" director John Sturges smashed through – to me anyway – how I really should have known better and whilst gaol was inexorable for me, I fundamentally learnt that the infectious camaraderie depicted in the movie among the POW's exists – in *droves* – in our country's prisons and is *totally* untapped and underutilised. Why not have a go at exploiting that in our jails? Inescapably Scrubs' suburbia has many *capable* people housed – an array of talent – many eager but languishing and shunned because of a system ultimately cack-handily managed with zero inventiveness by powers-that-be personage terrified of the purists.

It is the sworn duty of all officers to try to escape if captured during wartime. I was no Roger Bushell – or Bartlett, just a common convicted moronic thief. Having been barred within prison of doing *anything* productive – putting something back in, to coin the phrase, I set out overtly to try and fulfil my duty and do something constructive. The terrible inner anguish feeling of knowing full well that my dreadful behaviour was all down to me has somehow spurred me on to try and conclude some positivity from this whole nightmare.

The following is what happened during the recovery from that cauchemar.

The Agent

Dear Jonathan,

No, I'm not in Wales yet. I've read the first 7 sections of your book and it's most compulsive, which is what I said yesterday, the reader wants to read on and of course it's a very very sad story. I've printed off section 12 but may not have time to read the rest of what you sent before I go to Wales on Friday a.m. I will however take it with me and hope to get a couple of hours to finish it. I'll be back here on Monday early evening and will be in touch on Tuesday.

I'll be thinking about it when I'm zooming down the M4.

When do you think you can come up to London to talk to me? I assume you're very short of dosh . . .

I'm really looking forward to getting on with the book. It is a bit of a *tour de force* . . . AND you haven't spoilt your case by being too vitriolic about the prison officers and the whole set up. It's much more subtle and effective to let the story almost speak for itself.

I'm amazed you didn't go round the bend 'inside' – I really am.

The Visit

The very primitive looking machine had a telephone incorporated within it. It hadn't rung before, so when it did – robustly – I jack-knife jumped out of my jankers' skin. It was early on a subdued Monday evening.

The day of the week an important plot line by the way.

The electronic tag on my ankle and I moved to the source of the ear-splitting pealing with pit-stop priority. This contraption was after all my jailer. Not being sure whether I should be talking or button pushing – this thing had more keys on it than a prototype video recorder, I pensively uttered an uncertain hello.

"Mr Robinson?" Er...yes? "You're there then." Er... yes, I replied – for I was already armed with this information. "There are two officers at your front door, will you please let them in."

BLOODY *HELL.*

I *think* the receiver was replaced. The rather more pressing objective was to get to the front door – of the hostel – with gusto. This locomotion was concluded with *no* tooling around at a more than measurable Usain Bolt tempo. The ticker-tape of the front door reached, it was more than apprehensively opened, fulfilling the spectacle of a brace of unbranded uniform clad gentlemen from one of the companies that provides the Home Detention Curfew service to our Criminal Justice system.

"Mr Robinson?" Er…yes? "You're here then." Er…yes, I replied. One of your colleagues has just telephoned to tell me that too…

"Can we come in please?" A startlingly superfluous request as when on tag, as a still serving prisoner – albeit in the community – these gentleman and their organisation had firm grasp of the helm of all stage directions involving me. In they shuffled. I closed the front door of the modest three-up, two down town-house and we all awkwardly looked at each other in the hallway.

Like people do when in a lift.

Occupants of elevators rarely have the judiciary to send one back to jail. These two undoubtedly did. Any breach of curfew, it was back to prison for me. There was the most enormous thumping sound audible. It took a few seconds to ascertain it was the beating of my heart.

Beats in tempo followed whilst they eyed me up. Surprise that I was on the premises was displayed. "Can we see your tag please?" said one half of the duo with ropey-at-best enthusiasm. I proffered my ankle and as the grey plastic ringlet was displayed via the raising of my trouser leg, four eyebrows ascended vertically too.

"Oh," said the other in arid apathy.

"You still have it then."

Quite a lot of garbled information and explanation spewed out of me with angst. I've only just got out of prison, I'm fully aware of my curfew times, I intend to totally play the game, I have not done anything untoward and do NOT want to be sent back to jail.

"Let's go up to your room," suggested one of them "and have a close look at your tag." Up we traipsed, entrance to my bedroom was trundled and my cot reclined on. They poked around at my ankle-end grunting and murmuring like mechanics do at a local garage whilst diagnosing a clonking shock absorber. The most enormous cutting implement was produced. "Let's get it off," said the brandisher of the hardware.

Somewhat relieved post snip that he had been referring to their property and not my limb, closer inspection was made of the apparatus in a manner reminiscent of delving around the back of a fridge's contents after a night out. Much sniffing about ensued aided with comments passed similar to a debate on whether or not a sourced piece of cheese was still edible. "It doesn't look like it's been tampered with." It was time for me to voice more of my defence in pure panic – for my time on tag appeared to be on the skids.

I haven't touched it. I have been utterly punctual to sticking to my curfew hours. I haven't done anything… Am I in trouble?

"No, we can see that it hasn't been got at", said the one holding the tag – still sniffing it. "These things sometime pack up. Don't worry, we will give you another one and make a report – but you have been off-radar. Have you been here whilst you are supposed to be?"

YES.

"Hmmm," having another whiff.

If the machinery was saying I wasn't here – why didn't your lot phone me like they did this evening to tell me you were here?

Downstairs it was raised eyebrows. Now it's raised shoulders. Slow-burning embarrassment preceded the sublime fully flavoured Barnum and Bailey closing dialogue.

When did I vanish off your system?

"Saturday."

Post Expiate

Dear ____,

I hope this finds you well. I am sure that you have heard from the powers that be that I was released – under curfew – on November 21st, 2011. I have checked with the same bodies that it is acceptable to get in touch with you and they have encouraged me to do so.

I stress that I am not writing to you to satisfy any authority.

I could make this a very long epistle full of remorse and apology – of which I am full of, on both counts – however, the proof is in the pudding so I will cut straight to the chase.

I am sorry for the carnage caused by my behaviour. Please don't think for one second that it has not mulled in my mind. It has. Constantly. I have been through a very long process of transition in my ways of thinking. I understand it is now down to me to show – anyone interested – that I have indeed changed my ways. Suffice to say: I have.

Prison, taught me a great deal.

Thus I am writing to see if it is possible to formulate a plan with you to set something up along the lines of a payment plan to you. I hope that is the right terminology. I have various things in mind, of which I will happily discuss with you should you be open to sit down and discuss them.

I hope this letter is received in the spirit that it is written,

Jonathan

The Landlord

Jonathan Aitken flagged that getting out of prison is quite possibly harder than being put in. He wasn't kidding. Researchers have concluded that of all the pitfalls facing ex-jailbirds, accommodation is *the* priority. Re-homing is followed hot on the heels by unemployment and significant financial problems.

I won't even *touch* on the drug issue…

I simply don't know what I would have *done* without the hostel that Zara (Top) found for me. Apart from needing approved accommodation for the Home Detention Curfew I needed a roof over my head; a base. Without my stepping-stone lodgings, I would have served all of my punishment in prison. Zara (Top) you are in my hall of fame.

As previously recorded a temporary abode was required because during early days at HMP Bedford, my landlord had decided that enough was enough and communication was received that my tenancy was being terminated. I can't say I blame him.

My interlude of curfew was occupied with more than time consuming typing. Perhaps I have discovered the ultimate cessation of reoffending? Maybe all ex-prisoners should be barricaded and made to write a book. A newfangled take on days-of-old when schoolboys were punished with the writing of lines. As bashing of keyboard progressed, so too did the countdown to the end of the curfew – and the time limit of my allowable fortification residence in the hostel.

My measly collection of belongings and clothes were kept busy too. The months spent transposing IN IT were completed relying mouth to mouth on a bag of possessions no larger than one would take for a weekend away. Unquestionably, a gypsy way of life. I am not complaining. I caused the prevailing havoc. Besides, I had a book to focus on.

Imagine what it's like for those without something to get their teeth into.

Early efforts to boost my wardrobe supply – and enquiry of the status of my belongings – were executed by telephone to my ex-landlord. He was genial – to a degree – and proclaimed that he was happy for me that I was out of prison. Preliminary inquiries of any chances of moving back in were flatly rejected. This I acquiesce accepted so then posed if I could be reacquainted with my belongings. Yes I could. With one immeasurable caveat.

If I paid him money.

I – according to him – apparently owed for some months' rent for the period that I had been in prison – this was news to me. The rent had been paid up to date before my enforced holiday and the notice-to-quit received long before I had got anywhere near being familiar with the lay-of-the-land within Bedford jail. He was asked to email his version of events.

Over the following period – enough weeks to make months multiple – various emails ping-ponged with demands for a sizable sum, which I didn't have. Promised phone calls and texts were not returned by him and I didn't know what to do. I repeatedly sought clarification from him on the status of all my stuff. Months later an email finally came back which said: *Pay the money and then we can sort it out*. All this took place whilst I was still on licence and thus some very delicate manoeuvring was going to be needed so nobody could say I had done anything wrong. An ex-offender's inclination first port of call when he is having problems?

His probation officer.

By this point in time of proceedings visits to the not terribly inspiring – but always friendly – much of a muchness prison-after-sales department were every other week. As the crisply ironed shirt clad – always equipped with a lanyard – gentleman sat me down in a back office I asked if he could help me. He nodded perfunctorily and was brought up to date with the predicaments of homing issues and after voicing desperation I placed a verbal chit requesting if he could contact my ex-landlord as none of my telephone calls were being returned.

"No."

The thin edge of the wedge.

Plan B then. Books and paraphernalia in the local library were consulted, so too a free legal advice organisation. Both alerted me that keeping someone's possessions against their will were most certainly not Marquis of Queensberry rules. I pondered all this very carefully before deciding what to do next and came to only one conclusion…

I turned up at my old flat.

It was dusk and the place deserted – apart from my ex-landlord's car. I tried his mobile number and by good fortune – mine I suppose, not his – he finally answered. He sounded not overjoyed to hear from me. Even less so, when I announced I was on site…

"You're *here*?"

More than enough time for a sizable quota of French farce wardrobe door shutting elapsed before he appeared – flustered – and we convened in his office, adjacent to my old home.

I noticed various things of mine within his workspace.

I hadn't put them there.

The conversation's atmosphere was cool – and that's putting it mildly – but civilised. A start. I won't bore you with the full dialogue but the bullet points were would it be possible to sort out a payment plan and could I please have my possessions back?

"No. I want payment in full. Cash or credit card."

Attempt was made to make him understand that I simply didn't have the money. Surely he could be reasonable? That got me nowhere. A different approach was gently manifested. Was he aware of what he was doing was illegal?

"Oh yes."

Not much more was said.

I left feeling completely dejected.

Post-Mortem

Hi,

Victims react in different and often unpredictable ways to the receipt of correspondence from their offenders, no matter how well intentioned, and there is no way of knowing beforehand. I thought your letter came across as laudable and honourable. At least you tried and so you can move on and focus on putting your life together.

Miss Moneypenny

The pages written in prison doorstep-filled two lever arch files and it wasn't long before I realised that my typing tempo was not up to scratch. Things were taking forever so I opted to try my luck on seeking some help. An advertisement was placed on a free website for a typist – off the wall sense of humour, a must.

I only got one reply. Request for an email address was fired back so notification from the outset would explain that this was not a normal run-of-the-mill project. The beer-money pay was aired, so too a confession that the respondent was now communicating with an ex-prisoner. Expecting either a running for the hills or not-for-me reply what I in fact got was *"sounds fascinating."* A meeting was set up.

Lisa, my Godsend, made me laugh from the outset. She was also highly supportive of what I was trying to do. She had just had a baby, was stuck at home and I think climbing the walls in between feeds with non-utilisation of a very clever mind. She nearly had my hand off when I offered her one of the bulging files.

From then on I would receive sporadic emails – often dispatched in the middle of the night, with a couple more days typed up. Occasionally there would be a comment; *this bit is funny*, or *did that really happen?* What would really make me laugh though was; *I can't read your crap writing.*

A right little factory we became. I'd be bashing away at my end with the remaining file and Lisa did her stuff at the IN IT satellite office (night shift).

I think the productivity was 6:1 in her favour…

Lord knows how her little one – who is gorgeous – will turn out. Perhaps she'll be a writer after her formative months were spent with the incessant noise of typing in the nursery.

Aftersales Chaos

My initial hostel room-mates were a dream come true; sensible, house-proud, good company, respectful and admirably able to entertain the endurance of the presence of the tall posh one. They even put up with my peculiar habit of getting up at stupid o'clock each day as I fought to reduce the mountains of hand-written manuscript material as IN IT slowly metamorphosed. They had the patience of saints. The kitchen became mission-control.

Incidentally, I would share digs with either of them again in a flash.

All good things must come to an end however and the inevitable grinding of the system's conveyor belt took place when one of them moved out – jettisoned back into the community chest of society to start again on the Monopoly board of life post prison. The remaining chap – let's call him Scott (preferred prefix to anything from the milk supply being low, to Spurs' latest performance: "FARKIN' 'ELL") and I hoped the replacement incumbent would be of the same high quality.

We apparently should have put more effort into our hoping.

Alarm bells started to ring from the outset. Instead of a quiet first-night-out-of-jail evening with a can of beer and the telly, we were invaded. Youths in baseball caps armed with bottles of Jack Daniels peacock paraded the lower levels of the abode. Some even ventured to the first floor to sound out the action. All were very capable of producing more than half decent Ali G impressions.

Scott – the senior resident – was not impressed ("FARKIN' 'ELL") and sibilance vernacular normally associated with prison officers flew around like scattering birds as our guests were ushered off the premises. Following their departure he then ascribed the house rules to our new shipmate.

On the second night it became clear they had not sunk in.

Other people's utilisation of substances not available in Tesco is normally not my concern or business. However as a newly released, on licence, still sentence-serving under curfew, tagged jailbird – at large in the community – where giving someone a funny look on the bus could get me recalled to clink, my modus operandi did not include having white powdered concoctions anywhere near my vicinity – let alone under the same roof. This, though, is what reared its ugly head. Tonnes of it. We could have opened a dry-ski slope such were the quantities of the white stuff.

I retreated to my room to type. If there are parts of IN IT that are particularly wobbly, that's my excuse.

Again Scott read the riot act ("FARKIN' 'ELL") making it crystal clear that items had to be removed. This task was executed the following day and our new resident went about his business – literally – over the subsequent period in the local town.

This was to lead to his downfall.

His off-piste activities became of interest to the local police who I assume had some dialogue with the local probation organisation. What was to occur three or four nights later, and for the week after that, personified Billy Smart's circus.

I was fast asleep. I suppose it must have been about two in the morning. Scott's voice woke me. "FARKIN' 'ELL," was bawled from his – front of the house, the master bedroom – direction. By the volume of his transmission I deduced he was addressing someone outside. "FARKIN' 'ELL, HE'S NOT FARKIN' 'ERE. NOW FARK OFF!"

The crashing din of a window being whacked shut preceded his bedroom door being flung open and to the probable purveyor's room Scott stamped. Bailiff bedroom door knocking came next accompanied by lots of "FARKIN' 'ELL." Eventually two-way communication was established once he within sleepily answered. Scott steamed "the FARKIN' filth 'as just been FARKIN' well 'ere, FARKIN' looking for you. I don't care wot you FARKIN' done but sort it FARKIN' out. I told 'em you weren't FARKIN' 'ere."

There was a mumbled response. Scott then stomped back to his room and slammed his door. I lay in bed thinking…

Surely if we are all on *tag* then the system *knows* where we are?

I slept in the next morning. When downstairs was finally descended Scott moodily made tea. Our third man had departed early doors, I gathered. What had happened? "Four FARKIN' cozzers FARKIN' woke me up." *Four*?! "FARKIN' yeah. Three blokes – one was FARKIN' fat – and one bird. Oh, and a cozzer van an' all." Scott educated me further that this lot had arrived to collect and re-house our newly departed at the local prison. "FARKIN' recall, innit. I told 'em he ain't in and they FARKED off."

But he has a tag. Didn't the system *know* he was here? And the police just *left* without *checking*?

"FARKIN' system's FARKIN' FARKED, innit Jon. You wait – his FARKIN' phone will FARKIN' ring tonight…"

That evening at 1910 – ten minutes after the curfew activation, Scott and I were in the kitchen and indeed, a telephone rang upstairs. Scott raced to the source with me in hot pursuit – in case it was mine. It wasn't – the noise originated from the now vacant room. Scott scooped the cumbersome machine up, sat down on the empty bed and lifted the receiver. A voice down the other end asked if that was Mr_____, having noticed on his radar screen that the holder of that tag was not within proximity of the apparatus, de rigueur whilst on HDC during the appointed hours. Scott replied as belligerently as possible, grinning at me like a Cheshire Cat. "Nah." This threw the operator for a beat. Could he please speak to Mr_____? Scott: "Nah," and put the phone down, clearly absolutely *delighted*. "FARKIN' idiots," he decreed as we retreated back to the kitchen.

This happened again the following night.

And the night after that.

And the night after that too.

And – believe it or not – the night after *that*, as well.

Some evenings later at the habitual hour of the now regular phone call Scott put the hapless operator out of their misery. After answering and explaining that no, he wasn't Mr_____ he was asked again if Mr____ could please come to the telephone. "Listen FARKIN' numb-nuts, if you want to FARKIN' speak to Mr FARKIN'____ I suggest you call the FARKIN' prison because that's where he FARKIN' well is."

Thwarted, the caller at the other end frantically consulted the pointy end of a pre-printed manual for some form of procedure to follow. Scott went for the kill before slamming the phone down with pure triumphantly trumpeted glee:

"Sort your FARKIN' system out!"

The phone never rang again. About a week later a rather embarrassed female from the tag company turned up asking if they could have their machine back.

I'm rather glad she did.

Scott wanted to sell it on the FARKIN' internet.

Service

Whilst still on tag an appointment with another ex-prisoner was made for luncheon. I'm not mentioning any names (Dennis). A well-heeled location was nominated for this midday soirée and my dining companion was found punctually hovering outside an expensive looking eatery at the appointed hour. Entrance was made to a dimly lit space which would probably have made the late Michael Winner turn on his heel in an instant – such was the gloomy atmosphere. A thread of archaic piped music droned from some corner to add to the funeral parlour ambience. A snooty maître de in a suit that had seen better days cocked an uninterested eye at us as my host asked for a table for two.

A serene slothful scanning survey of the more than half empty dining area was made by him with the worn lapels and we were asked if we had booked. On negative there were some clucking noises, an irritated sigh and some stately head shaking. We were obviously a massive inconvenience to this gentleman. A booking-sheet was examined – and then more head shaking accompanied by exhalation of air over yellow teeth came our way.

My companion wasn't having this – and thus engaged the blockade so:

"Look mate, we've both just got out of *prison*. My mate's peckish. He gets *funny* when he's hungry. Got it pal? We want a table. And we want it NOW. Capiche?"

I have never seen a member of staff in a restaurant move so fast in my life.

Lunch was good.

Not surprisingly I suppose, so was the service.

Teevee

Hello Mate,

How's things, sorry it's taken a while to write, I'm now in a Cat-D and it's Alrite been here about 3 week I was in a 6 man dorm wen I first got here, it was like being at UNI campus LOL In a double now and got a job in the kitchens, so I'm eatin well. I'm glad you've got back on track wiv things and I hope everything well, and your still writing, in my dorm was a fella who been in 26 years and has writ a book for every year, "26 books". I've got some funny things to tell you anyway mate

Take care and good luck. Teevee

Iago

Dear Jonathan

I have read the pages of IN IT that you sent. You highlight a systemic problem within the prison service and its associated service providers.

We do need to ensure that we do all we can to prevent absurd situations like the one at Hollesley Bay to prevail unaddressed. I believe it is a crime to deny a life changing activity to prisoners because of personal prejudice. Your comments about the Head of Education will have an impact and something will be done to demonstrate that this is something the service does not approve of. It will, however, be seen as coercive and therefore create enemies.

RAMSEY

Did they give you a rough time?

BARTLETT

Not nearly as rough as I now intend to give them.

RAMSEY

Roger, personal revenge must be kept out of what we have to do here.

BARTLETT

[scoffing] *What my personal feelings are is of no importance. It is my duty to harass, confound and confuse them to the best of my ability.*

RAMSEY

That's true.

BARTLETT

Well, that's what I intend to do. I'm going to cause such a terrible stink…

Prison Service Orders

Order Number 1215 Professional Standards:

Preventing and Handling Staff Wrongdoing

The purpose of this Prison Service Order is to support a culture committed to high personal and professional standards, to set out mandatory requirements and guidance on preventing wrongdoing. This PSO supports the recognition that staff wrongdoing is an issue, and that the Service is committed to dealing with it.

House of Commons

Wednesday 22 February 2012

The House met at half-past Eleven o'clock

PRAYERS

[Mr Speaker in the Chair]

Fiona Mactaggart (Slough) (Lab): Since he has been Prime Minister, the company ____ has won contracts worth £224 million from the Department for Work and Pensions alone. In view of the fact that there are record numbers of unemployed people and that employees of this company have been arrested, what action is he taking to make sure that neither vulnerable unemployed people nor the taxpayer are victims of fraud by____ ?

The Prime Minister: The hon. Lady raises an important issue, which I understand dates back two years to schemes run by the previous government. As I understand it, it was the company itself that raised the issue with the relevant authorities. There is an ongoing police investigation, so it would be inappropriate for me to comment much further. All I would say is that the investigation needs to be thorough and needs to get to the truth, and then we can take its findings into account.

Investigation

The Daily Telegraph 29 February 2012

There are concerns that ministers awarded £440 million of new contracts to_____ and appointed its founder as "families champion", when officials already knew about accusations against the company.

Yesterday, the Prime Minister said he has asked the head of the civil service to conduct an inquiry into what happened. He also wants the Cabinet Secretary to find out if there are any other cases of financial irregularities that ministers are not aware about.

The founder of__, who received an £8.6 million dividend from the taxpayer-funded company, resigned from her government role and the company last week to prevent herself becoming a "distraction".

Allegations that former_____ employees falsely claimed jobless people had been placed in work are now the subject of a police investigation, which has already led to four arrests.

Mr Cameron clearly distanced himself from any knowledge of the alleged fraud.

Rod Redemption

Come the dénouement of *The Shawshank Redemption* Red finally locates Andy on some South Seas' benchmark Bacardi boardroom beach and a Hitchcock (*Frenzy*) helicopter shot closes the picture with their reunification.

Re-contact with *my* Red involved neither aviation steady-cams nor seascapes. A mere phone call rekindled our friendship – about a month and a half after I got out of prison. There was no doubt whom was on the other end of the phone when the potency of *that* voice was heard…

"Hello Biggles…"

Rod! How are you? When did you get out? Are you OK?

Being so thrilled to hear from him I didn't retain much of his response. He'd been released just before Christmas – when all the agencies are shut – and had been shacked up in some hostel or other. The grim stories reminded me again how lucky I had been in my temporary dwellings and the calibre of the other housemates. Rod's reflections didn't mirror mine at all. That was the bad news – the good news was that he had found a job on some building site. This was a *stunningly* superb accomplishment and noises of severe encouragement were gushed down the phone from this end. His good-conduct was questioned and confirmation that he was behaving himself was murmured.

As we chatted his voice took me right back to Hollesley Bay. He – bless him – wanted to know the latest on the book. Having been brought up to date it was agreed that once he had next been paid a visit to my locality was on the cards.

He said he'd stay in regular contact and I told him I'd kick his arse if he went off the rails.

I was so happy to hear from my friend.

RED

[narrating] *I find I'm so excited. I can barely sit still or hold a thought in my head.*
I think it's the excitement only a free man can feel, a free man at the start of a long journey whose conclusion is uncertain. I hope I can make it across the border.
I hope to see my friend and shake his hand. I hope the Pacific is as blue as it has been in my dreams.
I hope.

The Landlord (Part Two)

Having managed to face the music solo throughout my prosecution it was with great regret that professional legal services became required to resolve the return of my clobber. All my possessions were still being held for ransom by my ex-landlord. I thus found myself sitting opposite a young man in a local legal-aid funded advocate's office and spurted out my story. He was sympathetic. Did I still have the paperwork that had been posted to me in prison with the notice-to-quit?

Yes I did.

This was scrutinised with Holmes-like forensic precision by him and then came a glimmer of hope. "This isn't legal," preceded all sorts of eviction jargon which was more than Greek to me. A game plan was hatched. His ploy was two-fold: He would write a letter to the hostage-holder and I would make a formal complaint – to the police.

The local police station was enormous. I felt more than like Daniel entering the cave and took a number. The uniformed – but not a police officer – female behind the counter was trying to explain – ferociously – to a foreign gentleman that he could *not* sleep on the premises. The conversation was getting more than heated when two other people holding car insurance certificates nervously entered the establishment. Having taken their number, they joined me in the queue and observed more than bemused as the performance went on.

It was established that this fellow had spent the previous night here – following him being arrested – and now had nowhere to go – and could he please check in again? If his English was better he may as well have blithely asked for breakfast in bed and the newspaper of his choice. The what-he-saw as a receptionist made it very clear – more than theatrically – that there was no room at the inn. The potential house-guest departed the scene, no doubt to seek pastures new. Next it was my turn. If I hadn't already subconsciously gathered that this female enjoyed playing to the gallery, then it was about to more than dawn on me.

I misguidedly stepped up to the plate…

It wasn't quite "WHAT DO YOU WANT?" but that's close enough. Jail taught me that honesty is the best policy so I – tried – to explain that I had just got out of prison and was having problems with my ex-landlord.

"OH YOU'VE JUST GOT OUT OF *PRISON* HAVE YOU?"

It was *so* pantomime like that I half anticipated the car-insurance-certificate holders aft of me to chant *Oh no you haven't*. Sadly, that didn't happen. I acknowledged that yes, indeed I have and that I had been advised by a solicitor to come and talk to the police.

If they hadn't heard her at the back on her first broadcast, the cheap seats would have had no difficulty catching the contemptuous gist of her second proclamation.

"YOU'VE JUST GOT OUT OF *PRISON* AND A *SOLICITOR* HAS TOLD YOU TO COME TO *US*?"

I confirmed her assumption was correct. That earned me: "CAN'T HELP YOU. NEXT." I thus made good my exit.

I hope the car insurance documents were all above board – and that those clutching the relevant paperwork hadn't just got out of jail.

Tag Off

9 March 2012

There was no elation when they came. No rejoicing. I just felt stupid. The date of the contraption being removed from my ankle had been known for ages. The hour was uncertain – the paperwork stated it would be sometime before midnight. In fact they appeared long before the bongs of that evening's news and it was all very unexciting.

Up we ventured to my room and with a snip – my tagging days were over. The offending grey plastic attachment was removed from the offender and placed in what was either an evidence bag or something for keeping sandwiches fresh in. It could have been either.

The receiver contraption with the Del-Boy phone was scooped up and back down the stairs they went.

I thanked them and after shutting the front door made my way through the house to the kitchen. The back door was opened. The hostel had a garden. It had been walked about in before but never in the dark. For since being here – November – a strict curfew had blanketed me. Outside excursions after 1830 had not been on the agenda for the last four months or so.

The view from the open door was soot black. Unfamiliar fragrant cold night air charged at me like a fierce bull. The sensors in my skin questioned my brain (there's one there allegedly) as to the change in atmosphere. My decision making process questioned my locomotion. Until now stepping out was verboten. Brain told foot to continue and outside was trod.

This was an airlock.

My eyes – adjusting to night vision – focused on the end of the garden. There I walked and stopped, looking all around forcing myself to take everything in. Get thinking Robinson. Brain ticked over... consider what your traitorous Kim Philby behaviour landed you in... how lucky you have been getting off so lightly... most of the sentence was in an open prison... then the rest of it was in a hostel... with a garden... with beer in the fridge... I felt very guilty again, the paradox paralysing. It was a near full-moon as ghostly scudding slips of cloud danced across the winking lunar orb like blinking lights at sea.

I stood rooted all at sea. Absorbing. Mulling. This was the end of another part of the journey. I still had another seven and a half months of being on licence to tick-off but now the immediate restrictions were lifted. I was a free man.

Now the hard work was going to start.

BARTLETT

Open up Harry. We dig. Around the clock.

Iago (Part Two)

Hi Jonathan

I believe you are publishing your book at a good time. There is a growing public expectation that something different needs to be done to improve the way we rehabilitate prisoners. Historically, prison reform has not been vote winner. As a consequence politicians have been reluctant to go out on a limb to bring about much needed liberal reform. Prison reform is not a vote winner in itself but the escalating costs of reoffending and maintaining the custodial estate, at a time when savings are being demanded, the spotlight has and will continue to fall on a system that is failing to address unacceptably high levels of reoffending. Let's hope your book will fuel arguments for greater change.

Prison Service Orders (Part Two)

Order Number 1215 Professional Standards:

Preventing and Handling Staff Wrongdoing

The processing of information about staff wrongdoing is to expose and prevent corruption and wrongdoing in the prison service. This PSO is primarily about actions which may be taken to prevent wrongdoing and the handling of information that indicates or raises the suspicion that a member of staff is in breach of professional standards.

Moving On

No longer electronically monitored, the hostel – my approved address – was no more a mandatory abode and a new home was needed. I was told not to panic – they weren't going to throw me out on the street but could I please get busy.

The decision had already been made to stay local. The rents are low (quoting Neil Diamond) and the familiarity of the locale was inset within me. This also fell nicely into place with the baby-steps game plan that had been instigated towards the end of prison days. Local papers were studied and so too the internet.

And that's where I found it. A small offset one bedroom apartment that was well within budget. The pictures looked good; a newly refurbished kitchen stuffed with cupboards from that Swedish place that I always get lost in. A viewing was arranged.

From initial snooping – even outside – it was *perfect*. A private patio area too! Inside didn't need a map to find one's way about – it was miniscule. But it was spot on. A deal was done and I moved in a week or so later.

It was strange leaving the hostel – fleeing the nest. As I write this I smile about some of the things that happened there. I must pause and say thank you to both the people who run stepping stone accommodation for ex-offenders and – as the norm with the majority of my prison experience – my lucky stars. The hostel though, and the required time in it, had run its course. This Robinson Crusoe stepped aboard his newly acquired small vessel, hoisted the mainsail and cast-off on the next part of the voyage.

It didn't take me long to move. For someone else still had all my possessions.

Prison Service Orders (Part Three)

Order Number 1215 Professional Standards:

Preventing and Handling Staff Wrongdoing

Prison Service staff are expected to meet high standards of professional and personal conduct in order to deliver the Prison Service Vision. The Prison Service principals underpin the work of the Service and all staff must therefore encourage prisoners to address offending behaviour and work constructively with criminal justice agencies and other organisations – obtaining the best value from the resources available.

Staff must carry out their duties loyally, conscientiously, honestly and with integrity. They must take responsibility and be accountable for their actions.

Repossession

Having settled in to my new abode – the task of which involved unpacking three plastic bags – the legal lot who were in communication with my old landlord gently put the pressure on. It was hinted that a visit to the police had been made – totally true but completely unhelpful – but more vitally, suggestion was made that they were going to contact the powers that be at the local Council – the landlord police – and that they were aware my hostage holder of bags had one or two other properties out there. His actions; illegal eviction and possession of things not his, might not go down too well…

This did the trick. An email from him to my legal mob popped-up out of the blue saying I was more than welcome to come and pick up my things. This was the end of living out of three supermarket bags. This was also the cessation of demands of the thousands of pounds I apparently owed…

The legal-eagles told me very plainly not to make any funny remarks – just be nice as pie. This I was – and so was he – when I arrived with a Polish man and his truck.

BOY was it good to get all my stuff back. Clothes, pictures, electrical items and… well… all my DNA.

You have *no* idea.

There was some damage to this and that. Nothing major. No need to make a fuss. Onwards and upwards Robinson.

Rod Redemption (Part Two)

The train snaked out of the station as I heard *that* voice. "Hello Jonathan." Whilst other commuters passed us – striped shirts on some, trainers and windcheaters on others – I grabbed the origin of those words' hand and shook it for all that it was worth.

I hadn't seen Rod since November 21st 2011 when the roll-on roll-off prison system had spewed me out. He hadn't changed one iota – still a complete double of Jason Statham – except for what he was wearing. I don't know *where* his clothes were from but he looked like he'd recently been shooting a 1980's pop video – in East Germany – for Duran Duran. I was too polite (and thrilled) to see him to say anything other than it was simply fantastic to finally shake the hand of the person of whom in prison – with his boundless obvious abilities – I had just clicked with.

We walked up to my flat swapping information like Banshees. It was *so* good to see him. I reminded him of one of the many conversations between us in prison when I warned him there would be no fancy restaurants but death camp cuisine baked beans chez JR. He politely laughed, but cheered up a bit when I told him I had made an Italian meal and we were not reliant on Heinz.

Post meal the pub was ventured to. We didn't go mad. Just talked. And talked and talked and talked. You probably get the idea. I had taken my camera with me and got someone to take a picture of us. I still have that picture – I've just looked at it.

Encouragement was poured his way for getting out and getting a job, no mean feat. More progress than me – this numbskull solely preoccupied with writing – and asked him if he was behaving himself. His head went down for a fraction on the voicing of this headmaster's office query and out came some story of an altercation with someone or other.

I read the riot act, making it abundantly clear that he – and for that matter I – could not even afford looking at a Traffic warden in a funny way. I got a guilty schoolboy look in return and he acknowledged that he knew I was right.

We got back, a camp bed was made up for HRH in my living room and he asked if he could stick a DVD on. As I collapsed into unconsciousness in my bedroom next door I heard Rod chuckling to his film of choice; *Snatch.*

VINNY

What did you do that for?

TYRONE

I didn't see it there.

VINNY

It's a four-ton truck Tyrone. It's not as though it's a packet of fucking peanuts is it?

TYRONE

It was at a funny angle.

VINNY

It's behind you, Tyrone. Whenever you reverse, things come from behind you.

House of Commons

Tuesday 15 May 2012

The House met at half-past Two o'clock

PRAYERS

[Mr Speaker *in the Chair*]

Neil Carmichael: What measures can the Minister use to encourage the Shannon Trust's "toe-by-toe" mentoring scheme?

Mr Blunt: I recently met the chief executive of the Shannon Trust, and I assured him that we will continue to support his excellent scheme. I would be surprised if the new arrangements we have put in place for getting the commissioning of offender learning much closer to prisons and the institutions themselves did not see a much greater take-up of schemes such as toe-by-toe.

Fiona Mactaggart (Slough) (Lab): In view of the very poor performance in Ofsted inspections of provision by ___ , which provides much of the education in prisons, what conversations has the Minister had with colleagues in the Department for Business, Innovation and Skills about how, when the contract is re-let, the quality of provision and the achievements of the prisoners will be at the fore of decision making about who should provide it?

Mr Blunt: I understand that a written ministerial statement has been made today by the Department for Work and Pensions in respect of ___ which will be of interest to the hon. Lady and the House. In addition, a review of offender learning has been undertaken by the Skills Funding Agency. It was organised by the Department for Business, Innovation and Skills, and I am happy to say that its findings have been positive as far as ___ is concerned – I know that will be of interest to the House.

Government Ends Contract

The Daily Telegraph 15 May 2012

The government has terminated a contract with welfare-to-work firm ___ after deciding that continuing would be "too great a risk".

Employment Minister Chris Grayling said the company's Mandatory Work Activity contract to help up to 1,000 jobless people in the South East find work was being ended. The Department for Work and Pensions (DWP) has been auditing its commercial relationships with ___ after receiving an allegation against the company earlier this year.

"While the team found no evidence of fraud, it identified significant weaknesses in___'s internal controls on the Mandatory Work Activity contract in the South East," Mr Grayling said. "The documentation supporting payments was seriously inadequate and in a small number the claim was erroneous. There was also a high incidence of non-compliance with other relevant guidance (including ____'s own processes)."

"The process established prior to March fell significantly short of our expectations. As a result, the department has concluded that continuing with this contract presents too great a risk and we have terminated the Mandatory Work Activity contract with ___ for the South East. Contingency plans are in place to ensure there is continuity of support for participants in the Mandatory Work Activity programme."

The Writing MP

24 May 2012

As the arduous manufacture of IN IT continued an MP got in touch with me. News in prison reform circles spreads fast and through the grapevine he had heard that I was in the process of attempting the opening a new front on jail jitters. I understood he was doing the same – also in written format. Prison related books are apparently like buses. After dialogue with his assistant in Westminster revealing my *On the Buses* take, my mobile buzzed and I had lift-off with an MP for the first time on HMP. This individual knew his stuff – in a past-life he'd practiced as a criminal barrister and had been in and out of prisons all his life – in a professional capacity that is, unlike many of his wannabe cabinet-past-present-and-future contemporaries – the lot that don't ride bikes to Downing Street anymore.

Throughout the call there was a lot of could I help him with this, could I help him with that. No problem. I wanted 'in' with someone with clout. This could be a possible opening for me to the suits. He asked me to read his manuscript. I agreed and the nuts and bolts of the chaos witnessed by me whilst working for Her Majesty were barrelled through – met with sighs. A meeting seemed logical. At one point he said that he would like to set up some seminars with the both of us talking. Anything I can do to help, I responded.

From the outset it was help *he* wanted. I received an email shortly afterwards. Unedited it read as follows:

Dear Jonathan
Good to chat just now
Just to confirm - come to Portcullis House next wednesday at around 1.30. Take a tube to Westminster, come out of the tube and urn left and walk around the building Portcullis house is facing the river. There is security to go through - - once through ask at reception for me and they will call the office. I will be free for around an hour or so

What I need: longer term we can chat and discuss ways of shouting this stuff from the rooftops but what I am most interested in is:

any criticisms or errors in the book: if I am wrong then please say

Fisherman's News

"All the romance of trout fishing exists in the mind of the angler and is no way shared by the fish," said some rodman of repute. It was early evening when the phone rang – an unfamiliar number reeling me in. "Is that Jonathan Robinson?" said a voice that sounded like it should have spent the day bossing Hugh Fearnley-Whittingstall about on a trawler on some grey misty sea. Intrigued, and preparing to deny any knowledge, interest or participation in either fishing or poaching, I consented that it was indeed me at this end of the line.

What was to come next landed me hook, line and sinker.

"My name's ____. I understand you are a friend of Rod's. He's been recalled to prison."

The world stopped.

Details were sketchy to say the least. The caller was either being cagey or didn't know any firm details other than Rod had done something that had warranted his probation people to feel the need to rehouse him at HMP Lewes. Statham-man had got a message through to him to ring me, alerting me of this ghastly news. Rod, he told me, would be in touch.

After our conversation I felt nothing other than drained…

Of all the people I had met in prison Rod had been the hardest worker, he'd gone on – and *on* – about not wishing to go off the rails again and above all else – he had gained employment after his release.

What the hell had happened?

Scandal

The Daily Telegraph 26 May 2012

Pressure is mounting on the government to improve transparency over the firms it awards lucrative contracts to after ___ was accused by a whistle-blower of systemically misusing taxpayers' money in a "multi-billion pound scandal".

Written evidence submitted to Parliament by a former chief auditor at_____, a copy of which was seen by The Daily Telegraph, said an "unethical culture" led to "systemic fraud" at the company, which turns over around £215m a year through 72 state contracts.

The allegations came a week after the Department for Work and Pensions (DWP) cleared ___ of fraud in its current contracts. ___ denied any wrongdoing.

The Public Accounts Committee (PAC), said taxpayers deserved greater openness and transparency following the ___ problems.

The Writing MP (Part Two)

I am not aware of the quotas or statistics of how many on-licence-serving prisoners have been admitted to the bricks and mortar that is the Palace of Westminster but this minnow is one of them. Getting in made airport security look like toy-town. Guns were everywhere, loose change was x-rayed and Fort Knox formalities were relegated to sub-division levels.

I don't know *where* that would put our prison security in the league. Is there an amateur division?

I felt weird – though stubbornly determined to attempt denting the prison problem – but heavily out of place, like being underdressed at a dinner party. The architecture beamed Ken Adam atmospheric cantilevers of guilt my way. Belt up, I said to myself. This is a door-opening to the suits. Get on with it and turn your antennae on.

Into the fold I stepped.

My potential door-opener arrived. Short, but I understood he was an ex-member of the jockey fraternity.

As many members of Parliament munched lunch, predominantly particular personality pennants peculiarly portraying political persuasion, the MP and I chewed the fat on the subject HMP. Again it was could I do this – could I do that. Wanting to appear willing I eagerly consented – besides, I needed to test the waters.

It was agreed that I would consult other ex-prisoner colleagues on his behalf to gather as much information for him as I could.

In hindsight – that wonderful prison avoidance word – he was playing me like a Stradivarius.

There appeared to be an awful lot of common ground. He copiously scribbled notes as I recounted my fables. I happily sprouted off. Anyone with possible power for change had my attention. Nothing I said seemed to shock him. He was curious as to where I was with my book. I revealed that it was a view of prison held under a satirical scalpel – a tongue in cheek tilt at the true reflection of reality – and that I had been an events magpie in jail writing anything and everything down. If the book could open a new front on prison reform by admitting comedy into a grave situation – I would be a content ex-prisoner. When it was disclosed that Jonathan Aitken had agreed to write the foreword his eyebrows shot up. He wrote that bit down.

As our revolving door merry-go-round prison system was discussed a stunningly attractive girl holding an ice cream got stuck in one of the revolving doors that one passes through to gain entry to Portcullis house. It's funny how some things are noticeable to me. A policeman with a big machine gun released her.

Away from cornets and back to our confab: After I had voiced bullet points of some seemingly outlandish – to me – events experienced during my incarceration I navigated myself back to testing the waters. It was time to sound this gentleman out, did I have a toehold in Westminster? This was a litmus test. Now to tap the barometer. My insider-access question exuded no emptiness.

Why is the prison system so antiquated and why won't politicians do anything about it?

His answer was tumultuous precursor preparation for what lay before me in my battle for prison reform:

"Jonathan, all politicians are terrified of the *Daily Mail* and the prison issue is an election loser."

Red Letter Day

11 June 2012

Dear Todger…

Well mate what can I say, im absoletly gutted! iv done nothing. I had an aurgument on the Friday befor I come to see you, only a heated descusion and I wallked away, then I whent to probation as normal and she recalled me I dont no what to do im so upset and stressed. I <u>think</u> its a 28 day recall but it could be longer. iv been here one week from 6/6/12. iv got no numbers, cloths or money. im writing this but I ant got your address but my flat mate has found your number but my pin phone is <u>still</u> not working and I havent got any money on it anyway

whatever happens I should be out soon my main concern is keeping my job open and trying to make probation understand that nothing happened. I have no charges or evidence for that matter.

I could realy do with seeing you mate I feel very alone and sad.

iv been on 23 hour bang up all week iv put in for some peer support work and the kitchens. probation is ment to be coming up this week to do a report and I should have some idear by then on how long ill have to do.

I only had time to read the first bit of your book after you gave it me. can you photo copy it and send it to me please im hoping after reading it, it will remind me of who I realy am. I feel lost at the moment!!!

I should be getting out of my cell in a bit and hopfully my numbers have gone on so ill have spoken to you before you get this.

I feel absoltly sick as a pig. iv gone from having every thing to 23 hour a day bang up mid summer iv done 2 ½ years allready im afraide if they keep me to long ill loose everything?!?!

Anyhooz enough moaning from me I hope to speak or see you soon. im sorry mate.

Take care you Todger your mate

Rod

Prison Service Orders (Part Four)

Order Number 1215 Professional Standards:

Preventing and Handling Staff Wrongdoing

Managers must ensure that standards of behaviour and conduct are maintained. Staff must not have private interests that interfere or could interfere with the proper discharge of their duties. This includes financial and business interests.

Red Letter Day (Part Two)

Undated

Hay mate

Hope your well! im propa stugling iv only been here 12 days im still in shock. I will find out my fate next week im so fucked off and unhappy iv never felt so low!

I got £3 qid on my canteen sheet so I ant got no money to put to the phone to call you, things can only improve, I hope. im writing small to save ink, a trick I learnt of you, LOL.

iv got a feeling ill be here for 1 – 6 months? but im not sure I actualy feel sick all the time I just cant believe it!

I hope I see you soon mate take care hope your well your mate

Rod

P.S. I was in bed, its late I just woke its like 12.00 and *Shawshank Redemption* just come on the T.V.

it reminded me of you!

The Prison Officer

"Jonathan Robinson?" said the voice on the phone. On confirmation of this I gathered I was speaking to a prison officer who was calling to confirm that I was happy to receive telephone calls from one of his guests, namely Rod_____. Once I had agreed to this we got chatting.

The phone call lasted a good thirty minutes.

I don't know if he knew he was talking to an ex-prisoner, with my voice, probably not but it was made clear that I was familiar with the workings of prison and Rod's situation. He caught on that I knew my wings and landings – prison variety, rather than aviation circuits and bumps.

He didn't know why the recall had taken place – and probably wouldn't tell me if he did but did express positive noises when I said that Rod had been working hard since his release and as far as I knew had not been up to any shenanigans. It just seemed so frustrating that Rod had progressed upwards along the ladder but had now slid southbound on a snake.

"Contrary to public opinion," he said, "we do try to do our best for prisoners. We will do our best for him."

This comment ignited me. Whilst not venting my fury of being denied the opportunity to teach prisoners to read – in an open resettlement (?) prison by a private education provider, I did reveal what a travesty it was that it appeared most prison officers were poorly trained, not interested in anything very much and in the wrong job. His response surprised me. "I couldn't agree with you more. I've been in the service thirty odd years and all I have seen is a massive decline in standards." I sat up at that. The same hymn sheet had fallen open. We talked about how the role of the prison officer is as vital as a surgeon. Instead of him concluding the call he went further. "I tell you what; they're on the whole, a passionless lot now. But I'm ringing you – and other people – to ask if these prisoners can ring you up and right now it's my lunch hour. This isn't my job."

I thanked him and got off the line. I was impressed. There are some good officers out there…

Abysmal

The Daily Mail 28 June 2012

Scandal-plagued welfare-to-work provider, ___ has managed to get just 3.5 per cent of its jobseekers into long-term roles.

The company has already been hit by damaging allegations of fraud.

Its Chairman, who paid herself an £8.6million dividend in 2011 despite ___'s dreadful record, was forced to quit earlier this year.

The figures show that ___ – the second biggest provider of the work programme – is failing to meet its targets in the first year.

Margaret Hodge, the chair of the public accounts committee, which has been investigating ___ has said the figures were 'abysmal'.

Mrs Hodge said: 'We have had a relentless stream of emails, brown envelopes from people...who have worked for ___ complaining about poor performance, allegations of fraud and malpractice.'

House of Commons

Tuesday 3 July 2012

The House met at half-past Two o'clock

PRAYERS

[Mr Speaker *in the Chair*]

The Parliamentary Under-Secretary of State for Justice (Mr Crispin Blunt): Reducing reoffending is a key priority for this government.

Steve Brine: Does the Minister agree that there has to be a much greater role for offenders and ex-offenders in steering people away from the spiral of offending and constant reoffending?

Mr Blunt: I agree with my hon. Friend that ex-offenders are uniquely placed to offer support to offenders, along with other professional services, and can connect with them in a way that many other agencies cannot.

My MP

Hi Jonathan,

Further to our conversation. ___ will meet with you at our office on Friday 20th July at 10:30am.

My contact details are at the foot of this email.

Red Letter Day (Part Three)

11 July 2012

Dear Todger

Hay mate, just got your letter.

Thanks for sending me the pages (Author; Lines of dialogue from *Snatch*) I laughed my bollox off about the "pigs" it really cheered me up and it reminded me of lots of fond memorys to. We realy did make the best of a bad time!

I hope your well and things are going your way. i need you to know you have a very sobering influance over me, which I think I need.

im now working in the kitchens and on my way to becoming a peer advisor and a learner-support worker, and im also waiting to hear from my application to become a listener im getting gym regular and have a new cell mate and all this means im back to my old self and "nearly" fiering on all cillinders I could get shiped out any day to the Isle of white – Camp Hill (Great)

My MP (Part Two)

20 July 2012

Having made certain I was wearing a *blue* tie my MP's offices were arrived at. His assistant had been more than friendly on the telephone. As I had crashed on about my past inexcusable behaviour he'd stopped me, told me that the punishment was over and what I was trying to do on prison reform could only be a good thing – and yes – get over to have a chat.

The last meeting with an MP had been within the splendour of Westminster. This was different… Downstairs was stuffed with leaflets in countless languages and the adjacent sitting room had enough books – mostly on Marx – in it to more than make-up a Michael Foot honorary library.

Assistants to Members of Parliament at Westminster dress *Horse and Hound*. This example was clad à la *Exchange and Mart* but I immediately liked him. We drank coffee out of chipped mugs surrounded by the left-of-field books and talked prison-mess.

There was clearly common ground within what could have been the Greenham Common war-room of days past.

My MP arrived. You know how you're getting older when policemen look young? Jeez – I nearly offered my Member of Parliament help with his homework. If this MP ever transgressed the law – like so many of his contemporaries seem to do – they'd have to send him to a *Young Offenders' establishment*.

We sat down. I opened with my customary explanation of daft history past – something I promised myself I would *always* do whenever talking to *anyone* about the prison mess – it was *me* that got me in the jam – I was now just trying to do something about the whole lot of nothing I had seen – not – going on in clink. He asserted receipt of the abbreviated saga and straight away reeled-off statistics on our pathetic reoffending rates and the prodigiously expensive costs being hoovered away. He knew his stuff.

Let me be *very* clear now. I am totally aware that I landed on my feet in jail – being spat-out to an open prison with haste and then being tossed back at society so soon. The continuity of fortitude rolled-on with this meeting because to this day, this individual – and the team surrounding him – have been a pillar of rock to what I have been up to.

They could so easily have brushed me off but no, nothing other than complete and utter support – for this idiot. Like Zara (Top) at Hollesley Bay, my MP is in my hall of fame.

There was only one glitch. Prior to the meeting Meryl Streep's quite brilliant Oscar winning portrayal of Margaret Thatcher in *The Iron Lady* had recently been watched on DVD. In hindsight; a name *not* to bring-up when deep in the heart of Labour land. I asked my MP if he had seen it.

"I am not sure I could endure sitting through a film with *that* woman".

I don't think he was talking about Ms Streep.

Prison Service Orders (Part Five)

Order Number 4190

Strategy for Working with the Voluntary and Community Sector

Use opportunities such as mentoring to enhance interaction and understanding between staff and voluntary groups.

Red Letter Day (Part Four)

25 July 2012

Hello mate how are you? Its Friday night here about 8.00pm (early bang up!) im very board but cop(e?)ing ok. I moved wings from the dangeros retard wing (A wing) to a residental wing single bang up, clean, flat screen TV ect. Its much better, still working 7 days a week in the kitchen, as prison gose its all shit but I spose im top of the pile of shit, LOL.

im on an enhanced wing, being good. I got good reports and I even put in for my 'D cat'

im doing a open universty BTEC course, and making good of my time here on top of my pile of shit

Im going to write to mathew Kelly. Do you have his prison number?

Anyhooz hope your well and hope to hear from you soon. the pigs still make me laugh every time I think about it or read it, thanks

Speak soon your mate

Rod

OLASS 4 Contracts

The Skills Funding Agency

July 2012

The Skills Funding Agency has announced the list of providers for the new OLASS 4 education contracts for prisons, to start from 1 August 2012 except in East of England and London, where contracts will start in November 2012.

Following a successful procurement round, in collaboration with the National Offender Management Service, there were successful bidders for nine of the ten units of procurement. As part of the next stage in the procurement process, the Skills Funding Agency will now issue contracts to ensure delivery starts, as planned in August 2012.

Once contracts are signed, the Skills Funding Agency will apply its robust contract management processes, including quarterly performance reviews, working with the NOMS and lead governors. This enables continued assurance that public funding is being used and protected appropriately.

Prison Service Orders (Part Six)

Order Number 4190

Strategy for Working with the Voluntary and Community Sector

This Prison Service Order provides the Service with instructions on the management and development of an effective relationship with voluntary and community organisations. It sets out mandatory requirements and gives guidance on good practice.

PURPOSE:

Integrating the voluntary sector into prison work Making full use of the resources available

Red Letter Day (Part Five)

1 August 2012

Hello mate hope your well. Whats new out there? Iv had a strange few days, as you can see from my address, iv been transferd to HMP Camp Hill "C cat" prison on the island, but they have amalgimated the 3 prisons here, Parkhurst, Albany, and camphill. the induction wing is in Albany, we got to be here for 3 days or so.

this place is fucking strange the people here are long term sex offenders its so strange, me and 2 mates come over on the buss from Lewes and there are 5-6 other induction people here, to say we dont fit in is a understatment, this is the wierdest place iv ever been in my life!

I cant wait to leave here on Friday its a propa head fuck, there's some chapters for your book here I can tell you! no running water, or toilets in cell, not good im an hour from the mainland, Southhampton, I think?

its so strange, no one makes eye contact or mixes with each other.

the showers are on other residental wings.

Can you write back and let me know how you are and if you can get down at some point.

Anyhooz take care of your self and ill phone you soon your mate

Rod

PS Can I have a book of stamps please

The Cut

When an aspiring writer is lucky enough to get signed by a literary agent – he or she needs to listen *very* carefully to their wise words. Having finally got everything handwritten in prison into a computer – *something* of a story was showing – the Standartenführer demanded a cut. I fought my corner – I wanted the reader (would there be one?) to live every living breathing *second* of my time in jail. The Oberst's reaction: *Jonathan, people don't want to know what time you cleaned your teeth each day.* Then came some genius advice: *Take a break. Leave it for a while.*

Obstinate Robinson reluctantly closed-up shop and left the bally thing alone. Seeking distraction I got reading. And thinking. Right. Let's study how the pros tell stories…

Everything was read or watched. I got stuck into Dickens. Bios on David Lean, Alfred Hitchcock, Stephen Spielberg, Quentin Tarantino and Guy Ritchie were soaked up like sponges. Storytellers whose work I admire were studied. Films of theirs were viewed for the umpteenth time – with the soundtrack off but the director's commentary on. I'd spend hours microscopically mopping-up *anything* to do with Dick Clement and Ian La Frenais.

Boy, did I *learn.*

David Lean nailed it for me: *It's what you take out – not what you leave in – which makes a good story. Let the audience fill in the gaps.*

Hmmm…

A comment from Guy Ritchie hit its mark too. On one of his pictures he wanted to keep a lengthy scene in but the studio were pressing for a reduction in running length. Out the sequence went and the director realised it moved the story along better…

Hmmm again…

Back to work I went – and started slashing amok like a rampaging knight in armour. Following Joanna Trollope's sound advice, friends – the few I had left – who had been made to endure the first draft were redeployed to read early stages of the cut version. I only took out. I didn't want CGI to be added in post-production. It had to read real. Feel real. Be real. My take on calamitous clink in one take.

Everyone who read the abridged version reported back that it was miles better. Thus a full cut commenced.

Half of it went. Night became day.

The cut took me longer than I was in prison.

And was *much* harder work…

Red Letter Day (Part Six)

6 August 2012

Hay mate, just got your letter. Thanx for the old memorys, they was good times in bad circumstances.

im not in a good place this prison is naturiously pants! It is a book in itself unbelevably creepy and so strange!!!!! iv been about but I have <u>never</u> experianced anything like it iv got some storys to tell I can tell you! it is very hard to get off this island, my hopes are not high, to say the least!

I would very much like you to come and see me. im sending you a VO (Author: Visiting Order).

Can you send me the conker insident from your transcripts

I will write again soon take care mate and good luck with the edeting/slashing Take care

your mate Rod

Ken Clarke Refuses

The Daily Express 20 August 2012

Ken Clarke is giving the Prime Minister a headache over his upcoming reshuffle – by refusing to budge from his job.

The 72 year old is widely tipped for the chop as Justice Secretary in next month's anticipated reorginisation. Some Tory MPs want a minister who will take a harder line on prisons and sentencing.

Red Letter Day (Part Seven)

21 August 2012

Dear Jonathan

Hay mate! Hope your well. I trust you are hard at work with da book.

Thank you for the stamps its almost impossible to get free letters here. Thank you more for the conker story when I read the transcripts it takes me right back to the time as if I was there again, especialy the water pipe LOL! I remember how I was then and it seems apparent to me that my mo-jo has gone!? I need to get it back I find it hard to smile or laugh I am feeling very low and strugling to keep my head above water. Its just not knowing and the 670 days that may stand ahead it eats me away from inside, when I wake up in the morning its like a great wait lands on me and squashes away all hope. I know I "might" get out on a Parole Board but its hard to have faith.

The reason for my recall is that I was involved in an argument even tho I walked away I was still involved. My probation officer was concerned that I could have harmed the person I argued with. Im at fault for letting the situation get to the point of arguing and my probation officer was changing jobs and had to make a dession wether it could be a escilating situation and I assume she had to air on the side of caution resulting in my recall I supose she was just doing her job which is to protect the public and prevent any crime which on reflection I can see how it must have looked especially on paper. I hope they can now see that I am not a risk and having all these months to think about it I will be very awear of what I do and how I do it in future. I just want my life back. I would also like to think that it would be logical for me to have a period on licence when im out which will shorten my stay here. I am inhanced im a teachers assistant. im a R.C.C – which stands for Recognised Community Contributor – a peer mentor. I have all positive comments on my record approved accommodation, a full time job to go to, I have never missed or been late for an appointment and have done every course in the prison system. ther is not a thing I can do now but wait for my board.

Im starting or attempting to start an O.U. course to give me my supervisor CSCS card it costs £650 which I can get £500 of from PET the application is going through if I get it ill be able to get a top job, its sumthing that iv wanted realy badly for ages it's a realy good course and ill have so many more oppitunitys but the paper work process is slow

Anyhooz I enclose a VO. I understand it's a long way but it would be so nice to see you. When is the book coming out?

Do you have any details of anyone at Hollesley Bay I havent got anyones prison number I want to contact Mathew and Heston. iv wrote but iv got no reponse.

Anyhooz I hope this letter finds you well take care of yourself Speak soon

your mate Rod

Chris Grayling Appointed Justice Secretary

The Daily Telegraph

4 September 2012

Chris Grayling has replaced Ken Clarke as Justice Secretary, in a move calculated by Prime Minister David Cameron to delight the right of the Conservative party.

To the dismay of Liberal Democrats, Mr Grayling – a Eurosceptic Conservative known in Opposition as the party's right wing attack dog – replaced Ken Clarke.

Mr Grayling now takes control of prisons policy in England and Wales, as well as the courts system.

He has also made history as the first non-lawyer to be appointed Lord Chancellor.

His inheritance of the title as justice secretary was made possible thanks to Labour's 2005 shake-up of the judicial system.

The promotion to the Cabinet is a significant moment for Mr Grayling, whose stock fell in the final months of Tory opposition when he became known for his gaffes.

Red Letter Day (Part Eight)

Undated

Dear Jonathan

Hay mate hope your well sorry I havent phoned you, I just havent had any pin credit.

I got your letter the day after we spoke on the phone.

I assure you im doing things by the book and am being very good indeed. I still havent got a job in here and I STILL havent had any paperwork regarding my recall, its driving me fucking nuts.

I dont think I have got another sentence in me. I just cant get my head round it.

Tomorrow is my 26 day.

Its Sunday night been bang up since what was ment to be dinner (if you can call it that) at 4.30 – worst food iv ever had in prison, and that's saying something!

Reading your first letter, you say "make sure no one is writing a book" LOL you defo ant got no worrys most of the people here are not what you would call book worms, to put it very politely.

I hope I get news this week I can't fucking stand it here, its grinding me down day by day

Anyway thanks again for your support and allways be very weary of a man that keeps pigs!

your mate

Rod

Prison Service Orders (Part Seven)

Order Number 4190

Strategy for Working with the Voluntary and Community Sector

Every establishment will provide a constructive regime which addresses offending behaviour, improves educational and work skills and promotes law abiding behaviour in custody and after release.

REQUIRED ACTIONS:

Contribution of the Voluntary and Community Sector

There must be effective arrangements between the Prison Service and the Voluntary and Community Sector so that the contribution of the voluntary and community sector is focused, relevant and in support of Regime objectives.

New Prison Minister: Jeremy Wright MP

The Law Society Gazette 5 September 2012

After replacing Kenneth Clarke with Christopher Grayling as Justice Secretary, Downing Street confirmed this morning that Minister Crispin Blunt would also leave.

Joining the MoJ will be Jeremy Wright, MP for Kenilworth and Southam since 2005, who was called to the Bar nine years previously. Specialising in criminal law, Wright practised on the Midlands and Oxford circuit. He served on the justice committee in opposition and was made a government whip in 2010.

Prisons minister Blunt returns to the backbenches and has not made any public announcement concerning his departure.

Bedfordshire on Sunday

24 September 2012

More inmates at Bedford Prison have taken their own lives in the last year than any other jail in England and Wales. HMP Bedford headed the list as having the highest rate of suicides in 2011/12 with four prisoners out of the current population of approximately 465 offenders dying as a result of self-inflicted injury. The Governor at HMP Bedford said: "We are acutely aware of issues around prisoner safety. Staff are regularly trained in suicide prevention and we are able to call upon the expertise of a dedicated team who provide excellent care to prisoners in crisis. We work extremely hard to address the issues around safety in custody and as a service we save many more people through staff interventions than we lose."

IN IT Flashback

I've just been handed my French stick. There were two officers downstairs. One was supervising Angry Eyes and Ben as they dished out our supper, the other was the Walrus. He was in the mini-cab office.

And was *fast asleep*.

Prison Contracts Delayed

The Guardian

25 September 2012

The start of multimillion-pound contracts for the controversial welfare-to-work provider__ to take over education services in 25 prisons has been delayed because of the need to carry out anti-fraud checks.

The extra audit was ordered earlier this year by the Skills Funding Agency (SFA), which is responsible for prison education in England and Wales, after police began a fraud investigation into ___ and the Department for Work and Pensions terminated the firm's contract for mandatory work activity for the unemployed in the south-east.

The prison education contracts for jails in England and Wales that went to further education colleges began on 1 August. But the start of the ___ contracts for 25 prisons in London and the east of England were delayed until 1 November while the special audit of its past work in prison education was carried out.

The "comprehensive assurance audit" work was not completed until May and talks on the details of the contracts were delayed until the exercise was finished. The start date was put back from August until November "as a temporary agreement" and the existing contracts were extended in London and the east of England to ensure there was no disruption to prison education work.

"Through the audit work the agency carried out, the agency did not find any cases of fraud. Therefore it decided to proceed with the next stage of the procurement process in respect of London and the east of England, and to award contracts to__ ," the SFA said in a statement.

"As with all our providers, once contracts are signed the agency continues to apply its robust contract management processes, including quarterly performance reviews, audits and working with Noms and lead governors. This enables continued assurance that public funding is being used and protected appropriately."

The UCU, the university lecturers union, which represents prison education staff, said earlier this year it was difficult to see how ___ could be considered an appropriate provider after the DWP terminated its work programme contract because of "significant weaknesses in__'s internal controls" and ministers' comments at the time that it was "too risky to work with ___".

An ___ spokesman emphasised the audit had given the company a clean bill of health and resulted in a 0% error rate. The company said it had been involved in prisoner education since 2005 and had made a positive difference for thousands of offenders. It had over-performed against its targets for delivering qualifications since its current contracts began in 2009.

_____, the director of operations for Justice, said the company was delighted to have been awarded the contracts for the east of England and London: "This will enable us to engage and work with more offenders to help support them into employment on release, and not back into custody".

Red Letter Day (Part Nine)

3 October 2012

Dear Jonathan

Hay mate, just got back from the visit hall. I had to walk the long way so I didnt see you through the gate, missed lunch but im full of sweets and fizzy pop! It was good to see you, it really picked me up.

I know I need to start a carere and just concentrate on work. it is a sorce of ongoing termoil I battel with everyday. The job I have or had was a dream come true, I was so happy. im pritty shaw that they will take me back on, I was ajency but the bosses there all told me to apply to the MD and the job is as good as mine. I had also told my boss about my index offence and that I was on probation so because I was honest with him it should be my saving grace.

I am eger to get my supervisor/manager safety card. I have found a provider which offers a non NVQ based qualification, it has to be non NVQ based because it wouldn't work to try to get an assesor to come in and "test" me. its done in 3 moduals on thieretical senaryious – sienarioes (I cant fucking spell that word ®) ill try forneticly – sin-ar-ee- ows, anyway the PET – Prison Education Trust are paying for most of the £650 it costs, which is very cheap because most of the other providers charge 2 or 3 grand for the same card, everything has been approved and I am now just waiting for the go-ahead from the education department, but I will be very pleased indeed, just to start it, coz I can finish it, in or out most of the money £300 is for the card, which is a piss take, it lasts for 5 years and with this I could very easily find work that I love doing put with all my other qualifications it will be the icing on the cake work wise. in the hight of my criminal carere I has allways wanted to be a qualifide tradesperson incharge so I would give parts of my anatomy to get this so it looks like even though this has took the wind out of my sails some good has come out of it. It's the equivelent to your flying licence I supose!

You mentioned that you felt you had faild with your mentoring skills because im here, let me assure you, I have long been the most stuborn self destructive plonker you could imagen and no one to date, other than yourself has ever truly made me stop in my traks and take stock like you have. iv lost count of the times I have conciderd or reacted to a conversation as if you was there watching over me, when scull duggery was afoot. no one has really had the passion or influence to change me, but I feel looking back that I have allready changed and the recall was not realy a product of wrong doing but more a slap round the face resulting in a final tweak up of what I should be concentrating on and an oppotunity to galvanise my path what would have used to be temptation a year ago now dose not intrest me at all now. So from wher I sit your mentoring skills have allready worked and they have worked on a very stubon person on an exstream level, ie from a would be Bricktop to a ? well I cant think of a similar person because I dont have a full understanding of who I am yet but point is I have changed for the better and I have you to thank for it! So THANKS!

I hope to see you by the end of this month. thanks again for coming down, it ment a lot. take care of yourself

Your mate Rod

Conservative Party Conference 2012

Chris Grayling 9 October 2012

"A few months ago I was in the Clink. Not the famous prison in Southwark. But the prison restaurant which bears its name in High Down prison just a few miles to the south. It's one of the most innovative projects I have ever come across. A restaurant, open to the public, but where the cooks and the waiting staff are all prisoners, learning a new trade, getting ready for a return to the outside world, and with the real hope of getting a job. It's an inspirational project and a real example of what our criminal justice system should be doing to try to turn lives around.

It has to be a system which recognises that our prisons are full of people who face huge challenges. A system which is designed to ensure that they do not return to a life of crime when they are released.

We cannot deliver the reforms that are so desperately needed unless the public believe in us. I want to see more people who deserve it go to prison. But I also want to see far fewer coming back. The failure of our system to prevent reoffending is stark. Half of offenders are reconvicted within a year of leaving prison. Some reoffend within a matter of weeks, or even simply days, of leaving jail. Around one-third of offenders sentenced for indictable offences last year had 15 or more previous convictions or cautions.

You know what we do? When someone leaves prison, we send them back onto the streets with 46 quid in their pockets. Back to the same streets. Back to the same groups of people. Back to the same chaotic life styles. Back to the same habits as before.

So why are we surprised when so many commit crime all over again? It costs the economy at least £9.5 billion a year. It blights communities, and ruins lives. It is a national scandal. But the impetus to break this cycle is not just an economic one, or an issue of public safety. We know – and have known for some years – the factors which affect people's life chances. But the statistics – even if we think we know them – really are grim. Around a quarter of prisoners were in care as a child; just think about that. A quarter of people in our jails today were in care as children. I find that truly shocking. Nearly a third of them experienced abuse as a child; half our prisoners have no qualifications; half haven't been in paid employment in the year before custody; about two thirds have used drugs in the month before entering prison; nearly a quarter have a severe and enduring mental illness. Nearly three quarters of the prison population were identified as having either a severe and enduring mental illness, a substance addiction ... or both. These are issues we simply cannot ignore. We have to address them if we are to stop reoffending. I want to say to offenders 'We will send you to prison. But we want to change things so that you don't keep coming back'.

Inside prison, there will be more purposeful regimes. Maidstone prison for example has a textiles facility which produces work wear, and a laundry that employs offenders working a 33 hour week. There is plenty offenders can, and should, be productively doing.

Inside prison we must give prisoners proper skills and training.

When you think about the reality for the people who are in our prisons, you realise that we have absolutely no choice. It just has to happen.

I want to send a message to criminals that says 'we will send you to prison, but we will also help you go straight'. This is what I believe a tough, fair justice system should look like. This is what a revolution in rehabilitation should look like. And that is what we will deliver."

Red Letter Day (Part Ten)

18 October 2012

Dear Jonathan

Just got your letter. It lifted my mood as usual, you have been a rock of support and you have no idear how much you have changed me or how much I appreciate your friendship.

I am struling at the moment my fait will be decided in the next 2 weeks. I am beside myself with anxiiety!!! I dont know what ill do if they dont let me go.

The Prime Minister

October 2012

"In prison you will meet people who cannot read. These people need help. It's common sense. We will never create a safer society unless we give people opportunity in prison."

The Conservative Attack Dog

Inside Time

October 2012

What can offenders expect from someone who has been described as a Conservative attack dog and the jackal of the Tory party – with no legal background?

Red Letter Day (Part Eleven)

October 2012

Hello mate hope you are well. what are you up to now the book is done (is it finished?) Did you get the go ahead for flying, is that what your going to be doing for money? We could allways go into business and open up a pig farm but iv heard that you have to be very weary of a man that keeps pigs.

The last few days have been exstreamly hard for me. I keep getting upset for no exact reason. I think its a sign of depresion and my condition is exsassabrated by my pending release but I woke up today feeling much better. I do meditation from 6 till 7 o clock on Tuesdays and get healing from this Hindu guy it seems to work, there is only 2 or 3 participants and iv been one of them for the last 5 weeks. I know thats not your cup of tea So I wont boar you with the details.

Today I was working in the Paints and bricks workshop. I have took my role as a peer mentor and learner support worker very seriously indeed, in fact you would be proud of me, I can comnicate with people who are very dificult to work with, I mean teach or help, like dyslexic travelers and people who just never went to school. Iv managed to obtain placments for people on construction courses who dont have the required Lit and num levels which is against the rules but the education manager listens to me lots and people who would never get a chance to do these courses are now making progress in lots of differnt ways, which im proud of, iv helped change peoples lives and prospects, like I say you would be proud!

Cheers mate

write back soon as Rod

Licence Expiry

October 2012

The inevitable end of the road – the cut-off date for being a serving prisoner at large in the community – riding under the wing of a probation officer, eventually arrived. In fact, I was signed-off for solo about a week before the calendar conclusion because I was deemed safe in the community circuit. Back into the saddle of life I launched.

Being finally rid of the stigma of licence made me feel peculiar. The guilt of wasting the local probation office's time drummed home what an imbecile I had been. I have no issue with the compulsory attendance nor the reams of paperwork questionnaires we slowly trudged through on early visits. The problem is – and I'm not trying to sound big-headed I didn't learn anything. The culpability was heavily rammed home on each attendance whilst sitting in the waiting room with other also-rans. Most on-licence colleagues waiting for their box-ticking statutory parade clearly had mental health and/or drug issues.

My probation officer told me during one session that a member of his case-load was 'living with his partner – and their dog – in a van'.

I have just read what is above and fear I come over an arrogant buffoon. No matter. It is how I feel. I only so wish my time under probation had been more constructive. Just like prison wasn't. Maybe I would have felt better if after each visit a large bin-bag had been thrown my way with instructions to go and pick up litter. Something productive. A future chapter in this epic reveals how it was attempted to get some ex-offenders and a few members of staff to see a play that was running locally about ex-prisoners and their relationship with probation personage. Notion: Rejected.

Shortly after the Justice Minister told the world that he wanted ex-offenders to be 'at the gate' to meet newly released prisoners I turned up at my probation office – without an appointment – asking to see my manager. He appeared looking confused as to why I had appeared but agreed to see me for five minutes. In a back office I volunteered my services to him to meet anyone in his case-load who could do with a chat and a coffee with another ex-offender – this one – making it very clear it would only be realistic if anyone in that remit was 'sensible'. Someone not out of their head but who could do with a bit of encouragement from another who had the T-shirt, done the course. Notion: Rejected.

Before being 'released' I asked if it was possible to – at some point in the future – pop by and update the officer as to where I am. He knew about the upcoming book ("What are you going to say about probation in it?") and I had jokingly said I could visit in my Bentley. I also made it very clear that the whole project might easily fall flat on its face and I might end up road-sweeping down their street – whatever, could I stay in touch and let him know how I'm doing… Notion: Rejected.

In all fairness – the next time I saw him he rescinded that last one. He told me he had spoken to his manager and I could, if I wanted to, pay a visit sometime. I acknowledged this and thanked him. For the record, when I was finally dispatched by the services of probation I wrote a long letter to my officer thanking him for his time and efforts – and apologised that my irresponsible behaviour had put me into his remit in the first place. I also told him to stop panicking about what I had written about him. I reminded him – again – that he only really featured in the epilogue of IN IT, specifically when he and his colleagues had been on strike. His lanyard would always shake a bit whenever I told him that. He'd make me chuckle internally by saying "IN IT is a good title, innit?"

I suppose like anything in this world there are good and bad things. I have subsequently met with other probation bodies that are innovative enough to brandish offender art in their waiting room. Additional representatives in the field have remarked that they would have had my hand off to meet with other newly released prisoners. As I say – all things wise and wonderful have their bad apples… The helicopter flying instructor fraternity for example… prison education providers another…

I remember two visits to probation vividly. One was following a detour to one of those well-known coffee bars that seem to be sprouting up everywhere. Mostly on ex-bank premises it appears. I had sat in an armchair surrounded by very loud eastern Europeans doing their best to integrate into British society by wearing yellow footwear and turquoise tracksuits telephoning their home nation on one of their two mobile telephones in their mother-tongue. Invariably, very loudly. Opposite me sat a little old lady clad in tweed – an art director's paradise – who only just missed a *Lady Vanishes* casting director's dream-come-true by not knitting. She stood up to go. The cardigan was adjusted – then the overcoat – middle button first with an arthritic first finger and thumb. I was with laptop editing IN IT but I don't seem to be able to stop observing people… actions… *purses…*

She was a good six feet into making her exit when I spotted her purse had fallen out of her handbag and was tantalizingly in shot of an ex-offender. That's me by the way. On the success (?) of what you are now reading – this book – I categorically, *hand on heart* not ONCE even for a nanosecond considered *any* other action other than yelling for her attention. I *screamed* for the tweed. Even the eastern Europeans stopped shouting down their phones – albeit briefly.

She looked at me alarmed. I morphed into Basil mode and frantically pointed at the purse whilst hopping from one semaphore leg to another. "Oh, silly me," said the mixed flecked colours. "Thank you so much, young man". Up the purse was picked and off she tottered. No doubt totally unaware that her reunification with wallet had been strung- together by a serving-on-licence prisoner.

I left the coffee shop to it and duly turned up at probation. The story was relayed to my manager and he disappointingly (I thought – but I can see his point) asked me if I had considered keeping it. *No way in hell,* I protested. I'm not sure he believed me.

The other visit to my masters that sticks was one time my regular officer was otherwise engaged. I got a locum. A female. I'm afraid my nostrils more than flared – I could *hear* the breath decamp – on her vacuous opening gambit: "When was you here last time?" Biting my tongue I answered all of her indifferent questions but what galled was that she plainly had no idea of my case history or where I was in the process. I ticked the boxes and got the hell out.

Hindsight makes me wonder if either the little old lady with the purse or the probation officer who only just about knew my name – or both – were *tests* to see how I reacted before I was issued with my walking papers. Probably not. Far too innovative a game-plan from my experience.

Prison Service Orders (Part Eight)

Order Number 4190

Strategy for Working with the Voluntary and Community Sector

There should be greater consistency across the Service, with a well-managed relationship that allows space for local flexibility and the use of innovative approaches and ideas. Prisons should be proactive as well as reactive.

Holiday Camp Jail Perks

The Daily Mail

29 October 2012

Outrageous prisoner perks look likely to be axed in a shake-up of cushy jail rules.

A full review – the first for more than a decade – will examine the lax regimes which allow inmates to lounge in their cells all day, watching daytime TV or playing video games.

Prisons Minister Jeremy Wright told the Daily Mail he was worried too many inmates were routinely handed 'privileges' they should have to earn through good behaviour and hard work.

Currently, prisoners enter jail on a 'standard' regime, which automatically gives them certain entitlements, including in-cell television. They are only bumped down to the basic regime if they step out of line. Each prison devises its own scheme for how privileges are handed out.

Inmates can 'earn' entitlements to in-cell television, more visits, higher pay when they work, the right to wear their own clothes and access to their own money. Inmates are offered a string of digital channels, including: BBC1, BBC2, ITV1, Channel 4, Channel 5, ITV3, Viva – a music channel – and Film 4.

One option under consideration would be to start inmates on basic and force them to work for extra perks.

There have been complaints that prisons have become too soft and young criminals treat them like a 'holiday camp'.

Chief inspector of prisons Nick Hardwick said that on a visit to Britain's largest jail, Wandsworth prison in south west London, workshop facilities 'stood almost empty and too many staff appeared indifferent about the prisoners in their care'.

Red Letter Day (Part Twelve)

17 November 2012

Dear Johnathan

Sorry I lack the ability to spell your name, I cant help it! I hope your well and that life is treating you good, im trying to remain positive and doing everything I can to turn this situation around

Im just going to look at it as its likely ill get out around the middle of next year May June, ill have 11 months to go then and i should have completed the Courses they say I should do, the only problem is that im assessed as unsutable for these courses because my risk score is so low its madness

iv got my D cat review in a few weeks and im trying to get to ford which is the same as Hollesley Bay. I need to look into learning options in the local area, its in Bogner Regis, so I need to look at the collages and stuff because it increases the chances of me getting there, my heart is set on doing the Supervisor and Management course from the Open Universty, funded by the PET, if I get it I will be so happy it will make this stay almost worth it, thats how much it means to me, because I know when I get out I will be able to go to work and excel in things I love doing and ill have the proper qualifications to do so and get good money for doing it. I can say with hand on heart that I will happly do a year in prison if it means I can walk through the gate with that superviser and managment card it will bring evey qualification I have got together and will be the start of my proper carere!!! Just the thought of it excites me.

Anyhooz ill leave it there mate hope all is well and ill speak to you soon take care

Your mate Rod

House of Commons

21 November 2012

Jeremy Wright: In addition, my hon. Friend may be aware of the work of the Shannon Trust's "Toe by Toe" reading scheme, which is also available in prisons. Again, this scheme uses peer mentors, supported by volunteers, teaching staff and prison officers, and it is based on best practice developed through teachers' experiences of enabling children with dyslexia to read. That is enormously beneficial to many offenders.

Red Letter Day (Part Thirteen)

December 2012

Hi mate hope your well. Had a bit of good news, they have granted me an oral hearing! I havent got a date yet but it will probably be between now and January.

I only found out yesterday, it's a very good sighn indeed, people often get out on oral hearings. Im now excited.

Incidentely it's a training day today and im banged up all day, its nice to break the routine but im board as hell!

I will keep you up to date with developments and ill phone you when I can. Take care your mate

Rod

The CAA

During the journey of laborious lobbying (a *lot* of door knocking had been going-on) various friends – when one is down, one *really* finds out the pecking order of pals – started to poke me about returning to flying. Ex-students and professional pilots would all sporadically have a nag. What really startled me was that on more than one occasion someone would get in touch seeking aviation advice. They must have been very desperate. Like when answering flying questions in prison, I would surprise myself with how much information had been retained in my black box.

The stock answer was that I had to finish what I had set out to do – to get something done about the lack of encouragement for prisoners trying to teach others to read. I wouldn't be able to live with myself until this target had been reached. Swanning about in helicopters was not my priority – until a negative had become a positive.

This decision was reluctantly accepted – but as various flight-crew bits of paper with my name on neared expiry, it was ascertained that something needed to be done. Assorted helicopter companies were approached. Those that knew me blanked me. Eventually someone suggested I contacted the CAA – the aviation management.

I ended up speaking to the top helicopter boffin – who knew me. He had heard assorted speculation of the JR history but was nowhere near up to speed on the whole story. All was revealed. He was kind but very guarded. This gentleman was unaware that I had been debriefed by some of his colleagues the day after my release from Hollesley Bay. He explained that some backstage digging needed to be done and that he would get back to me. This was executed and the roster required that my presence was necessary back at CAA headquarters for a meeting. I could have someone accompany me if I wished. The offer was declined – I had nothing to hide. This was accepted and a request made that I attend armed with my flying licence and log books – my personal flying history, that all aviators must keep.

Crikey was I nervous as I stood outside the building – habitually occupied in yin and yang grandeur by personage replete with blue suits, brown shoes and monstrous comb overs. "A bunch of *failed airline pilots*," as my late helicopter pilot uncle used to refer to them. After a millionth cigarette, suited and booted, into Blofeld's volcano I went armed with no Q branch gadgets, only my wits – which I have no shame in admitting I was well and truly scared out of.

Whilst not strip searched, the security to get into this place was a lot more thorough than landing in HMP Bedford – Ahem, HMP Management – and a scanner had to be passed through. I'll say it again. *Ahem…* Once in, the helicopter boffin materialised in record time dressed in a suit – blue. I *did* feel special… After telling me that I looked older than he remembered he led this lamb to the slaughter assuming the mantle of a tour guide explaining that we were to have conference with the *senior* boffin. I was just trying to stop shaking.

A *real* David Brent scenario was entered. Within, a gentleman that resembled a fan of mealtimes – who wore too many gold rings. A female assistant loitered too – frantically trying to look busy scanning files – one of which was upside down. She would have no problem earning her keep as an extra in the film production world. He with the Ferris wheel rings shook my hand and welcomed me. I was to call him by his Christian name. The female in the room it was spelled out to me, was here to take notes. A non-speaking part then, a support artiste on the studio floor…

In heritage hindsight, I was not on set but what amounted to a court.

You know those Public Accounts Committee meetings you see on the telly? That's what it was like. I was *grilled* by the jewellery wearer as the boffin pulled my paperwork apart. They only just fell short of shining a lamp at me and asking who my resistance contacts were.

I sang like the proverbial canary. The whole nine-yards were laid out including my offence, my shame, that I felt like an idiot, the impending book and how I had learnt my lesson. I made it abundantly clear that I was not looking to return to aviation now but was covering myself before various ratings expired and that if and when I reached my self-induced goal of sorting out illiteracy in our prisons, maybe I would feel better about myself and then perhaps return to aviation.

Various questions and comments were made. The primary of the former was did I intend to pay the money back. Efforts to execute this and communication to my old boss were passed – together with the reaction. "It's written-off then," The jewellery-clad interrogator decreed. I firmly responded that my door was still open on that front. The comments – or hints – mumbled, seemed to indicate that because I was not a murderer the CAA would at least entertain the notion of my returning to instructor duties – but with some conditions. The caveats were that if indeed I was to re-enter the flying arena then they would want to keep an exceedingly close eye on me – I immediately consented to this – and again exclaimed that I had learnt my lesson. I even said it was my intention to not even get a parking ticket in my future law-abiding manifesto. The second prerequisite was that they wanted ten names and numbers of people who knew me – so they could really look into where Jonathan Robinson was. Again I agreed to this. "No ex-cons though," were to be on the call-sheet, said he-with-the-gold bands. This was acknowledged by me. The final demand was that all email correspondence must be copied into the female present – who sat in the corner logging on a yellow A4 legal pad, all that had been communicated.

Goldie stood up, indicating that the meeting had concluded – and gave me his card. As I was thanking him for seeing and listening to me, the helicopter boffin apologised to the lady-writer-logger that the conversation hadn't been 'more juicy'. This caused her to laugh.

It was the only sound she yielded.

Iago (Part Three)

Hi Jonathan

You do wear your heart on your sleeve and your openness has been refreshing. Also I do not question your passion to bring about reform in the penal system. I am happy to say what I can to the CAA should they contact me.

Carry on Doctor

With my new home came a new Doctor. That's not to say 24 hour medical coverage was to be found next to the freezer but a local GP signed me up. Charming he was too – and concerned about my hand. Dupuytren's contracture had long before prison been diagnosed – a tissue disorder that makes one's fingers curl in, painless but it slowly impairs grip. I have subsequently been informed I inherited it from Viking ancestry.

Somewhere within me then is a seafaring piece from the 8th century…

An appointment came my way – via text message – to attend a hand clinic at the local hospital. After the hustle and bustle of the waiting room (which smelled of perfumed disinfectant) my hand was prodded, poked, picked at and played with. My palm read that surgery was on the horizon.

More appointments for further tests were again texted to me – I never got anything in writing – no complaints from me, we live in a cakewalk digital age and having been seen by nearly everyone from medical students to ward cleaners I at last had a consultation with the surgeon who was going to do the hacking. A lady. From Spain.

I don't think she knew what to make of me. I have a dreadful habit of cracking terrible lewd schoolboy jokes in times of crisis and I fear most of them went over her head. Or she just perceived I was an idiot.

Patently ignoring the patient's unfavourable smut, she patiently explained that the procedure would be carried out with me conscious – and that I'd be of no use to anyone for about six weeks post op. The concept of not being given a general anaesthetic got my attention. I'd far rather be off with the fairies and not know anything about it but tough-cheese – this – resolutely – was the agenda.

I presented myself on the notified day – received by text again – at the appointed hour shaking like a leaf.

Various Hattie Jacques Matrons and Staff Nurses mother-hen clucked around as I was ordered to get changed into theatre gear and lie on a bed. Recalcitrant protestations that I wasn't tired and offers of did anyone want to join me, true to themselves, fell like lead balloons. The poor staff. Whatever they get paid – it's not enough. As per the norm when the pressure's on, I had my overly observant ears on – wary of the Barcelona butcher – and noticed each time that anyone consulted my notes that they'd look at me in a *very* funny way.

In between strange glances, someone promulgated that the anaesthetist would come and have a chat with me soon. A man. From Spain.

Pedro – that's what I'm calling him – was a *very* close friend of Dorothy. A scream. Camper than a row of tents and incapable of conversing without one hand on his hip. He made Larry Grayson look butch. I – although very nervous – got a fit of the giggles talking to him which he thought devoutly amusing. His back-up team, all stood behind him – and English – caught on when I asked him if he was Julian Clary's Spanish cousin. An errant epidemic of stifled hysterics erupted from the erstwhile equerries. Pedro didn't get it – and instead gave me a burlesque blossoming breakdown on the 'block' he was going to give me to numb my left side – all disposed with limp wrists akimbo. I was nearly chewing my lower lip off trying to stop laughing as he pranced on. The other team members all furiously polished their stethoscopes daring not look anyone else of the esprit de corps in the ethical eye. This just encouraged Pedro more. I feared he might start singing Judy Garland songs at me. Narrowly he didn't – thank God – but did say – shamelessly, "who is going to be a BIG BRAVE BOY then?" On that, two of his team had no option other than bolting for the exit for apparent fear of wetting themselves at the medical mincing.

I was then given something that I can only equate to three double gin and tonics – not-for-tourists measures. A nurse – who had drawn the shortest straw – was sentry seconded to my bedside to guard the off-his-face patient. I can't remember the conversation with her. I don't want to. I do know what was publically declared was utter rubbish. I was smashed. I do recall she had a moustache.

A team of heavies arrived. One wore a Sesame Street theatre cap. This was it. Still trolleyed, off I was trolleyed for the block. Some side room reached, Sesame Street asked me to confirm my date of birth and the procedure I was due for. A birthdate making me 21 and breast augmentation was merrily mused. "Can be arranged," said Big Bird's friend as Pedro and partners got busy on my left arm – with accompanied Spanish suggestive statements. The numbing – completely painless, soon put my whole left side well and truly into siesta mode.

Into theatre I was wheeled, the stalls stuffed with tiers of staff all dressed in green. A huge upper circle science fiction lamp hung above like Auric Goldfinger's laser. The irritated dress circle Spanish surgeon tentatively tapped her scalpel as I questioned if this was an Iberian conspiracy in retaliation to the Gibraltar situation. I don't speak her tongue but a morose mumbled monoglot monosyllabic mournfully muffled momentarily from behind the moody matriarch monolith matador's surgical mask. She muttered that she was in the company of a moron.

For the squeamish among you, I won't go into grisly detail. There was no pain at all. I made sure my gaze was firmly planted to my right side and the nurse with the moustache who kindly held the non-numbed hand as what seemed like a cohort of green attended the other half. The number of people in that operating theatre was humbling. Everyone doing their stuff for me. This jackass. Most were female. Because of the on-going gin and tonic effect I think they were all asked out for dinner with discernable desire.

An hour later it was over. Out I was taken – still plastered – after gushing huge thanks complete with a plaster cast. Later whilst sitting up in bed drinking NHS coffee a nurse tentatively approached with paperwork to give to my GP. I had a quick glance. No wonder I hadn't received any written correspondence and no wonder all the staff had looked at me so *oddly* on arrival. My address indicated I was still residing at HMP Bedford…

Red Letter Day (Part Fourteen)

Undated

Dear Jonathan

Its allways so good to hear from you, your letters allways kick me back into reality and rational thinking, when left to my own devic I sometimes end up in a dark place. I concider myself lucky to have such a friend as you.

I hope you are on your way to a full recovery and gain use of all your exstremitys!

As to my hearing it was sat on the 30/10/12. I got the ansew about 20-11-12. no recommendation to release! they said they think I need to do I qote "offence based programms" and in the same paragraph says that iv been assessed as not sutable for offence based programms so it contradicted its self.

The next opportunity for a hearing im guessing will be 6 months from 30/10/12 which works out April 30th ish which is only 4 months away, so I wont be home for Christmas. I will be happy to be home for next Christmas at this rate!

I have 17 months left and am in my 7th month. I am working very hard in attempting to do all the courses that I cant do and making a VERY good impresion with my behavor, Peer mentoring teachers assistant.

I got your post card, its pined to my wall staring me in the face as I write.

Im trying to imerse myself in learning. I do lots for other people, in the same way you used to do for me, in the hope I can change some peoples lives for the better and keep the good calmer.

I will phone you again soon but money is tight espeaclly with Christmas, ie lack of wages coming up with the Christmas holiday.

hope your better soon take care and thanks for everything your mate

Rod

House of Commons

December 2012

The Parliamentary Under-Secretary of State for Justice (Jeremy Wright): It is a great pleasure to respond to the debate, and I congratulate my hon. Friend the Member for Hexham on securing it.

The debate is not only important but timely, because the government will soon be publishing our plans to make a radical change in how we support the rehabilitation of offenders. My hon. Friend is rightly concerned with that new focus on rehabilitation both in this debate and in his excellent book *"Doing Time: Prisons in the 21st Century"* – no doubt available in all good booksellers and an excellent stocking filler. I congratulate him. He has eloquently set out today the issues that face us in tackling offenders' problems with literacy and substance misuse. Both are significant causes of offending and reoffending.

I want to ensure that prisoners have incentives to engage in positive and constructive activity during their time in custody. I want to ensure that we have a system that encourages offenders to engage with the support we offer, as my hon. Friend said. I am aware, as he is, of the difficulties that many prisoners have with basic reading and writing. We are placing a strong focus on assessing prisoners' learning needs and when a literacy need is identified, we make every effort to identify that as early as possible, and learning providers in particular have a responsibility to do so. Other things are being done to target prisoners with literacy problems, and to incentivise them to address those issues. We are working with education providers to develop engaging and motivating courses to target resistant learners particularly. Those courses will be marketed by prison staff as part of the prison induction process. My hon. Friend the Member for Hexham talked about the Shannon Trust, and he is right to recognise its significant contribution. I fully support its work, and have met its staff for discussions, and I am sure I will do so again.

We are committed to the use of peer mentors to support reading schemes such as its Toe by Toe project, and my officials are looking at how prison staff can better support its work.

Red Letter Day (Part Fifteen)

14 December 2012

Dear Johnathan

Hi mate hope your well, hows the hand? do you have any exciting plans for Christmas?

Christmas means a week of no work and all day bang up so im in for a tough ride till the new year.

Iv just got my canteen sheet it's a double one to last to last till next year but it wont last, it's all going on tobacco!

I am now waiting for a date for my oral hearing that has been approved on the 30/11/12. Should be January, iv been reading through all the paper work and it is looking good and im confident.

Wish me luck, ill write again soon

Take care your mate

Rod

Prison Service Orders (Part Nine)

Order Number 4190

Strategy for Working with the Voluntary and Community Sector

Mandatory Action: Involve voluntary groups in the development of policy and programmes. Ensure relationships are consistent and well managed. Promote and publicise partnership with the voluntary sector.

Red Letter Day (Part Sixteen)

Undated

Hi mate

I have moved! To Albany it's a B cat and full of very strange people. I was getting greaf at camphill, and didnt want to get into any trouble so the powers that be moved me. I do allready feel better and less stressed, only now can I see how stressed I was, iv losed wait, iv been here 2 hours! But I do feel better and as an added bonus I will probably get moved to a C cat prison on the main land if I dont get out on my oral hearing in about 6 WEEKS!!! I cant beleve how boged down with stress I had become. Only problem is now I have no JOB meaning no income for a few weeks which will be hard.

I have had confrimation that I am going to have an oral hearing, the date is not set, they have told me Febuary, which is only 5 weeks away, thank God! they accsept that the reasons are desputable so I got a good chance!

I am a bit un-settled at the mo but im ok and have gained back the will to live! Thanx for being there mate!

Until we meet take care and I hope you are well have a good Christmas!

Your Mate

Rod

The Old Boys Club

I don't know who saw who first but we recognised each other.

The road was immediately crossed and my hand out was stuck out. The reward was a big grin and "how are you Jon?"

I bump into ex-prisoners all the time. I will always stop and have a chat – maybe a quick coffee – and pose how things are going. They always seem grateful that the tall posh lanky **** is interested.

Prison taught me so much.

Red Letter Day (Part Seventeen)

25 + 26 December 2012

Dear Jonathan,

Hello my friend, thank you for your letter, I hope you are well and having a good Christmas

I find the transcripts nice to remenis on at the time its hard to appreciate how good them days wher, didnt seem so at the time but the more I looked back the more it becomes apparant that in a strange way they was good times, even tho we was "banged up" Im pleased that your recovery is going well, I have recoverd from camphill and have now gained back the will to live! seriously I was in a bad way in there!

_____has sent me a parcel its in reception, but I dont think they will let me have it I think its trainers and cloths, I had some Nike air max but they'v warn out and soak up water with every step so I got a pair of pedophile clasics from the gym im waiting for my amber light to go green so I can use the toilet and get water, I get 7 gose a night that must not exceed 7 minutes.

In other news the night befor I left camphill the young lad (22) opporsit me killed himself strangled with his green sheet and my flap was open a bit and I see and heard everything. Very nasty.

By early January the recall office (PPU) will be functuning again, the relavent info I need is the date of the oral hearing, which is yet to be set, they sent an e-mail on 20-12-12 to probation but then withdrew it the next day it said that the oral hearing was the 13-1-13 my OM then phoned and they confirmed that I was getting one but they have to set a date possibly Febuary so I think it's a case of the squeeky wheel

So ill be staying here on parole hold so if you was able to come and visit you would be a sight for sore eyes

Take care Your mate Rod.

The Justice Minister

1 January 2013

By email.

Dear Mr Grayling,

With your recent announcement of a mentoring plan for ex-prisoners I decided now is the time to write to you – striking whilst the iron is hot if you like. I emailed your predecessor in early 2012 but never got a response. I hope you accept the following epistle in the spirit it is written. I desire change – not trouble.

Whilst I fully admire the reforms/clean sheet of paper you are bringing to the table, no one has addressed the fundamental problem of the complete shambles *within* prison. Thus I am getting in touch with you.

I will try and keep this concise and will kick-off with some background information on me: Idiot middle class helicopter pilot steals money from employer to impress wife. Gets caught. Gets put into prison (HMP Bedford) on July 25, 2011. Wife leaves him. Gets moved to a Cat D five or so weeks later and leaves HMP Hollesley Bay on November 21, 2011 on HDC.

During which, a book was written. Sort of Adrian Mole in clink type material. Day to day life inside, for someone who had not been to prison before and who was rather a fish out of water. And some. Above is the latest mock-up for the cover. It was shot at St Albans Register Office and may be familiar to you as it's the same set of doors utilised in the opening titles of *Porridge*. The irony of that is that when Dick Clement and Ian La Frenais had the show in development they were allowed *into* HMP Brixton for research but *not* allowed to shoot the doors. Someone did some searching and found some good 'prison doors' in Hertfordshire. Thus this is the second time they have been used for a parody of prison…

I learnt a GREAT deal about myself whilst working for Her Majesty. I rapidly cottoned-on that I was among people who didn't judge me – but just took me at face value. Murderers, failed bank robbers and drug dealers all accepted me and taught me it was OK to be me. Much of the book – designed as both a deterrent to prison and that within prison that the king has no clothes on – is the journey of discovery made, via a great deal of bumbling, by yours truly. A recurring topic within the very dull pages is the relentless kicking I gave myself that it took to getting to the age of 46 and 17 weeks in stir to learn this very basic ingredient to decency.

It is also, quite possibly, the world's longest love letter and apology to my wife.

About half way through the shoot – it felt like a film production – I bit the bullet and wrote to Jeffrey Archer seeking advice as to what to do with my potential bird-cage lining. He very kindly wrote back, directing me to something called the *Writers' and Artists' Yearbook*. A steer to bother the agents that are literary was suggested.

96 letters went out – 'The Great Envelope Escape' – we were only supposed to send one second class letter a week though the system.

A great number said – via standard letter – 'Thanks but no thanks'. Curiously, 11 said that they would like to have a look. Two, with most enthusiasm. One of those, wrote to me more than my wife did.

Which was not at all.

I also wrote to other ex-jail birds – the notorious ones anyway – seeking guidance. Fellow cons had to rearrange my tunnelling duties around a great deal of pen work. Jonathan Aitken wrote me a stupendous letter back in support, and a great deal of correspondence has occurred subsequently.

The first agent who read it signed me. Now that's mentoring… The author Joanna Trollope, who came to HMP Hollesley Bay to give a talk on writing (!) advised me to get as many people as possible to read it before it was submitted. I asked Jonathan Aitken (among others) to have a read. He kindly said yes. *Unbelievably* (to me) he has agreed to write the foreword.

There is an episode in my piece containing *unbelievable* behaviour by a certain member of staff who frivolously squandered available (free) home-help with perverse virtuoso. The potential for prisoners to transform rehabilitation themselves is huge. I saw it sunk before me. Literally sabotaged from within.

Events were *Shakespearean…*

IN IT shows a very damning view on the warehousing of prisoners and I am afraid to report, what seems on the whole, a staff that isn't really interested. They were given the moniker of clock watchers early in the piece. It got worse – I found an officer asleep on duty on two occasions. Everything was documented. And I mean *everything*. One officer spent about 45 minutes at HMP Hollesley Bay telling me about the awful morale.

Another member of staff – who did have some gumption – came up with a very valid quote 'that a Cat D prison won't be a Cat D prison until it has Cat D prisoners in it'. When I asked another sensible officer how certain individuals had made it through the filter he very openly said it was because most of the prisons want to get rid of the trouble makers and sex up their records.

There are an awful lot of people in prison spending their days watching *Jeremy Kyle*.

I saw more drugs in Bedford than I have in my entire life. Some youngsters are getting themselves put in prison on purpose to make money...

Please don't think that I in any way surmise that I should not have gone to prison. Quite the contrary. However, a playing up car does not fix itself by being locked in a garage. The prisoners I talked to – at length – all *want to work*. I learnt that there is (some) *great* potential in *some* prisoners. In the current Luddite climate, not a lot is being done to nurture it. By all means punish offenders – but make them work hard and reward them (it's called *leadership*) when they do well. The size of the flat screen TV adjacent to the pool room on E wing at Bedford was obscene.

I am trying my best to mentor a prisoner who is currently a guest of HMP Camp Hill. I visited him in October. It was most strange returning to prison. In hindsight the staff there were very polite and seemingly efficient. This, despite me arriving initially at the wrong place (although I went to a sign that said 'Visitors report here'). The comedy in that was that the female (?) officer had forgotten her glasses and yours truly had to read the roll- call for her... Why does everything – by accident or design – happen to me? When I got to the end of the list having read out names like Slasher Sid and Basher Perkins I questioned why neither my nor the chap I had come to see moniker's featured on the call-sheet. Realisation set-in that I was not where I was supposed to be... Once we had established that I was indeed in the wrong prison (story of my life) she directed me next door and told me to "climb down the wall next to the prison wall" as a short-cut. As I was doing this – *surrounded* by CCTV – I wondered if I was going to end up in accommodation next door to my friend's...

On a serious note, as I was searched by staff (no problem with that at all), I got the sniffer dog treatment (and chastised for talking to the dog who was *sweet*), my watch was examined and so too the inside of my mouth. I had no problem with any of this at all but what has struck me is that this procedure was as a *visitor* to a Cat C establishment. My point is that as a *customer* on my arrival at HMP Boots the Chemist – sorry, HMP Bedford (Cat B), they *didn't bother* with any of this. And the place was *awash* with drugs... AND I WONDER WHY...

Whilst I was still in the remit of probation, a touring theatre company visited my town with a play called *Release*. An award winning drama about three recently released prisoners and the troubles/pitfalls/adjustment facing them post prison. When I suggested a visit to the theatre might not be the daftest of ideas for some ex-offenders and maybe a few probation officers and that it might open up some unused mental territory, the gentleman from probation looked at me like I'd suggested we all got tooled-up and went to Barclays with stockings on our heads.

A few months back I met with _____ MP who asked me to contribute to a book he has written on prison reform. _____ and I are reading from the same sheet of music. He has informed me that he has used the material I supplied to him with my recommendations and observations.

It was *most* odd attending the House of Commons for that meeting... I was still on licence. Lots of MP's were eating joints of beef the size of small family cars. _____ and I had a sandwich. He paid.

To summarize, I deserved every hour, minute and second that I served in jail. I should probably still be in there. On being sentenced having accepted that my life was now adrift, full of anxieties and fearing the very worst, what in fact met me did not finish me off, it simply exasperated me. Despite – with a very hard landing – firmly placing myself among baddies, the villain(s) of the piece are unequivocally the guileless staff, consummately huddling under the leaky umbrella that is the system.

Since my release much reading-up on our prison system has taken place. Nick Hardwick's last report on HMP Bedford praises the library (and its tiny annual budget, of I think £6000). It's interesting that he picked up on this. The Chief librarian was the only person I encountered doing her job with any real passion. I hope the piece reveals the enduring impact this had on me.

I learnt with horror in September of 2012, that during 2011/12, Bedford Prison had the highest suicide rate of any prison in England and Wales. 4 inmates committed suicide at the prison during this period, out of a population of 465 inmates.

I have also subsequently learnt that our prison officers are trained for something like eight weeks. Their colleagues in Norway are on the receiving end of a course that lasts two years…

If you survey the public (and I have) what *they* say is 'punish them – and stop them reoffending'. EVERYONE is saying – with much austerity – that the existing system isn't working. When is SOMEONE going to grab the nettle? Does it really take a third-rate book written by an idiot to shake the branches? It's fundamentally agreed by-one-and-all that the king has no clothes on. For goodness sake someone sit the likes of Danny Boyle, Sir Richard Branson and individuals with noddle down and re-jig the strategy with a (very large) clean sheet of paper. Having had my finger both in and on the pulse, the existing system is spewing out prisoners essentially having just let them brood, whist advocating a philosophy empty of ideology.

There is much film assimilation in my piece. If I have managed to transmute that our HMP management are – with panache – doing the equivalent of dubbing Rin Tin Tin then I have anecdotally attained my goal.

I am writing to you to you because I am determined to influence some change and would much rather have 'bigwigs' on my side… Please let me know your thoughts. I would be *very* pleased to talk with you. IN IT, out this year, is a plea for *change*.

The Walrus and the Carpenter
were walking close at hand
They wept like anything
to see such quantities of sand
"If this were only cleared away,"
They said, "it would be grand!"

Yours Sincerely

Jonathan Robinson

The Justice Minister (Part Two)

55 Minutes Later

Just to assure you, I did get it and read with interest, and have given also to Jeremy Wright my prison minister.

Best wishes

Red Letter Day (Part Eighteen)

14 January 2013

HMP Monster Island

Dear Johnathan

Hello mate hope you are well, I got your letter, I am OK, my mood dose go up and down tho, I may have bi-pola?

Yes it was very sad about that fela topping him-self, I didn't mean to sound bla-say about it, it did effect me, it was the night befor I left camphill and I could see them with the body bag through the door, on the night I did get very upset and sad, he was just to young to go like that.

Camphill has closed everyone will be shipped out within a month, the exidous has already started!

If Im not succsessfull at my oral hearing (which I think Iv told you about) I to will be moved from here to a 'C' cat prison on the mainland, I should be sucsessfull on my board tho, if SO I will be released about Feb 15th Im very nervous but will be very well prepaired for my board, as in organised.

I started work in the talors last week its shit, a sweat shop, there's some VERY naughty people here!

I just hope they dont "try" and move me befor my board, its possible my O.U. course is strugling to follow me, I really really want this qualification it will garantee me work, its got as far as the P.E.T. but my file is still in Camphill! I will endever to do it on the out if not but I must have it

glad your hand is nealy better. all I have here are thoughts, I often think of you and how your doing. I am finding "things" exstreamly difficult there is no one in here to talk to, especially the stuff that's going on in my head. iv managed to keep it together this last 9 months but im finding it increasingly difficult to cope, I cant put my finger on it. its to do with brain chemestry, I think, iv been up and down, as in my mood, but recently very down which is expected in here! but I keep getting very emotional and cracking up from time to time each day is getting worse. I fear im on my way to a nervious break down, seriously I dont want to make a big deal out of it for probation/parole so I gota hold it down till I get my anser at some point in febury I think I can do this, im also going to go doctors, I am turning into a nervous wreck! I don't want to be subject to the 5 year rule, that we descused some time ago!

Dont do anything with out my concent I just need a friend to talk to, the people in here, well the least said the better.

I must wait till the board Feb 8th and 2 weeks for the result, I don't think I will be able to cope with a knock back, they say ill be on anual reviews if unsucsessfull?!

iv lost 4 ½ kg in weight, I will get through the next few weeks, then I will phone you with the outcome. Dont want to worry you but im not in a good place and I never felt this way befor I feel like im fad(e?)ing away.

The Prison Reform Trust

5 February 2013

Committee Room 6, House of Commons

The Chief Executive of NOMS

Michael Spurr: There has already for some years been competition in prisons. We have got a very clear agenda about what we want to do in prisons, which is to focus on rehabilitation.

The Justice Minister (Part Three)

5 February 2013

Dear Mr Robinson,

Thanks for sending the foreword to your book through to the Justice Secretary, which he has now forwarded to me.

I have read it. Coincidentally, I had a fascinating meeting with Jonathan Aitken last week.

I would be very grateful if you could send me the whole text, as I am interested to read your reflections on prison and rehabilitation more fully.

Thank you again for taking the time to write to Chris. He is very committed to reforming the system, and likes to hear from those who share his passion, and who bring an important perspective to bear.

The Writing MP (Part Three)

Dear Jonathan,

I hope this finds you well.

___ has just organised a book launch for *Doing Time* on Thursday 7th February and wondered whether you would like to come? The launch is not for the benefit of parliamentarians as we have already promoted the book around MPs and particularly the Justice Team, but more for interested journalists and individuals from the law and justice world. If would be great if you are able to attend, especially after your input and help.

The launch will consist of ____ giving a short and informal speech about the book followed by drinks and nibbles.

The details are as such: Date: Thursday 7th February
Venue: _____ Street, London Time: 6.30pm for 7pm.
It would be great if you can come and I hope to see you there!
Best wishes

My RSVP was lobbed back with Andy Murray inertia. Trying – again – to be helpful, I inquired if he had invited various 'names' that are involved in prison reform whom further to my beating down of doors I now had contact details of. Said addresses were requested so various high-flyers' details were transmitted back from my little black book.

The nominated night arrived and having positioned myself in light rain rather too early somewhere near St Paul's with an hour or so to kill, a pub was sat in.

When one is a broke newly released ex-prisoner, one can make a pint of beer last an *awful* long time. Polite sips were supped by Billy-no-mates as the minutes dwindle dripped away. A freebie newspaper was read at a table below an enormous television attached to a wall.

The flat screen telly was nearly as big as the one on E wing at HMP Bedford.

Is a glass half full or half empty? During contemplation of this a gentleman asked me if he could occupy the vacant seat the other side of the table. I told him to help himself and he sat down with half a pint of beer.

Opting to give it five more minutes before leaving – I did *not* want to be the first to arrive, the chap opposite got up and departed having consumed his half measure of ale. He did that thing with his eyebrows to communicate "thanks and 'bye" that English people do when they are too embarrassed to say anything.

I vacated the pub shortly afterwards. The road stuffed with rush hour traffic was crossed in the still persistent precipitation. Finding the location, a legal bookshop, in I went. A meet-and-greeter hovered within who invited me to descend the stairs to the basement – where the event was taking place. Down I went. Fortunately, a good ensemble had already assembled and being relieved that I was not the pole-sitter, the MP spotted me, brandished a big smile and walked over and shook my hand.

"Thank you so much for coming, Jonathan. I've used a lot of the material that you kindly gave me. How's your book coming along?" I replied that it was a pleasure to be of help, that I was delighted to be invited and that the launch of IN IT was a couple of weeks away. As these facts drew to a close a figure descended the stairs – someone who had a terribly familiar face… Good God… I've never met this person before. I know him from the telly and the papers, he replied to my letter in prison – and some emails have bounced backwards and forwards but I have never encountered him face to face…

And he's just written the foreword to my book.

Jonathan Aitken looked more than a bit concerned that this six foot four buffoon had bustled up. Especially one who said 'hello Jonathan, I'm Jonathan.' It took a second or two for the penny to drop. Fortunately, when it did, his face lit up. He was as kind and supportive to me in person as he had been in all previous correspondence. He remarked that so few people who do end up in jail have the articulation or ability to communicate what is so horribly wrong with it and laid-on yet more encouragement. His memory was pin-sharp – asking how my hand was following the Dupuytren's contracture procedure – which of course his past boss, one Margaret Thatcher, had also been on the receiving end of. Weirdly, so too President Reagan.

Connecting with that duo, he revealed that he had recently been in the company of Mikhail Gorbachev, interviewing him for a forthcoming biography of Lady Thatcher. The last General Secretary of the Soviet Union was I learnt, 'fascinating' and 'very funny'.

As the Jonathan two-hander reached its conclusion, our host took to the floor to make a speech.

Everything said was more than topical. The key issue raised (from my point of view) was that perhaps the Ministry of Justice should consider dangling a carrot to illiterate prisoners that if they learn to read, some form of remission would be rewarded. He underlined that it was a proven fact that illiterate prisoners who do learn their ABC's, are less likely to reoffend. At this point he asked Jonathan to say a few words – then after telling the room who the tall bloke was – and the title of my forthcoming book – I was invited to say something.

If memory serves me correctly, I solely referred to the Shannon Trust, its Toe by Toe peer mentoring scheme and what wonderful work they – try – to do in tackling the horrendous problem of illiteracy in our prisons. I did not speak of the shooting-down of it that I had experienced during my sentence.

But I did later in the evening.

As the chit chat concluded huddles of people stood around with their glasses of wine – like they do. The MP neared and said he wanted to introduce me to someone from the "organisation that runs prison radio for inmates". It's a small world. The gentleman who shook my hand was the chap with the half pint in the pub. We grinned and I explained to our host that we had met – well sort of. Quick dialogue was had with this individual and then the MP – being an impeccable host – wheeled me towards two ladies "who are involved in prison education and I know that's up your street Jonathan." Introductions were made, I was introduced as the prison author and it was explained to me that these females were from some company that I had never heard of.

They asked what the book was all about. A précis was delivered and then a *bombshell* dropped. A real blitz. One of those Basil don't mention the war moments.

This duo were from the cumulative centre of the company running the education services at Hollesley Bay. The company being paid a hatful of money for doing so… The company whose employee had ordered me to cancel a constructive activity proven to reduce reoffending – that the *system had trained me to tutor*.

Dawning on me that I was behind enemy lines it was firmly – but politely – explained that my forthcoming book didn't make their organisation look terribly clever – and I had their farcical Head of Education more than in the crosshairs of my aim. They looked taken aback. One of them said "Are you gunning at just him or our whole company?"

Let's see what the reaction is to events when the book comes out, said I.

The other one announced that she was a director of the company – then started talking about 'delivery' and 'customer feedback'. I felt like I was having a conversation with some travel agent following a disappointing two weeks in Majorca.

The Justice Minister (Part Four)

8 February 2013

Dear Jonathan,

Thanks for sending this over – it makes for interesting reading, and I am glad your book is receiving a lot of interest.

I did get in touch earlier this week, and as I said then, am very keen to hear your views and read your book in full. I appreciate that you have sent over a list of things that you would like me to agree to before sending the text – and I just needed to give some thought to how we are best to take this forward. I do apologise that I have had a busy couple days, and therefore did not respond straight away. I can assure you that this is not through lack of desire to engage, or indeed to improve the system.

I will give you a call later today, if that's convenient for you. Apologies again.

It Weren't Us, Gov'nor

11 February 2013

Hi Jonathan,

When we spoke on Thursday evening, you suggested that your forthcoming book would mention some activity at HMP Hollesley Bay relating to ___ delivery/employees, based on your recent experience as a learner in the prison, and which would not be positive in its portrayal.

___ takes a proactive approach to all customer feedback – be that from clients, funders or other stakeholders. So, I'd like to understand who/what this relates to, in order that I can pass it to the relevant colleagues to investigate further and deal with the matter as appropriate thereafter.

I'd be very grateful if you could send me any relevant details or information about your experience at HMP Hollesley Bay.

However, if you wish to make a formal complaint about any of the services delivered by _____, you can contact our Customer Service team directly. There is more information on our website (www._____), but the easiest way to do that is by phone (0800_____) or email (customerservices@_____).

I wish you every success with your book.

Prison Service Orders (Part Ten)

Order Number 4190

Strategy for Working with the Voluntary and Community Sector

Responsibility at Senior Level in establishments: Mandatory Action:

Governors, Area Managers and Head of Groups must: Give responsibility to voluntary and community groups. Ensure that the quality of support and services offered by voluntary and community groups is of as high a standard as possible. Put in place systems that are sufficiently flexible to allow work with new groups and to test innovative methods.

The Writing MP (Part Four)

A telephone call from the recently published MP thanking me for attending his event and for contributing data and quotes for his research. The conversation was humorous and conclusion made that prison reform was going to be no overnight success. I asked him a straightforward question – seeing as he works indirectly for the management.

JR

Did you have to get approval from the Kremlin before publication in case you rocked boats?

MP

I can't really answer that.

JR

Well I assume if you had got too close to revealing the chaos they would not have been best pleased, so I guess they had the opportunity of giving your piece the onceover before it was printed?

MP

Er...

JR

I tell you what – I'll say something – and if you say nothing back, then I'll know they had to have a look first – agreed?

MP *OK.*

JR

The Kremlin had to have a look first before you went to print.

MP

Silence

Red Letter Day (Part Nineteen)

16 February 2013

Dear Johnathan

Please excuse the paper, I have just found your letter dated the 5th Feb it had been slid under the door across the floor and underneath the cubord. im sure you remember the stile of incoming post, it was just luck that I found it when I did!

I sat my board on the 8th Feb it went very well. it was very positive and I left feeling it was in the bag. They told me I would be informed inside 2 weeks, it has been 9 days so far, I can't stop thinking about it and going over it again and again I will know by this Friday! It is doing my head in badly! im not sure I could take a knock back, but im certain ill be released on Tuesday wednsday or Thursday im focused on my carere and am going to take life seariously

You have kept me sain, on the right path and give me hope when I have needed it the most, thanks for just being there, I will always be greatfull. Soon as im of this god forsaken island ill phone you on the way home, if I still have one.

Again thanks for just being there I pray that I shall see you next week, my fait is already seald in some tray somewere it just has to get to me.

See you soon

Your mate

Rod

Teaspoons

19 February 2013

The Post Office Tower is called something else now. A bit like the Labour Exchange is now known by one-and-all by some acronym or other. Whatever its new title I loitered outside it smoking a cigarette dressed in a suit. It was a glorious morning and not for the first time since lighting up, checked the hour. About fifteen minutes remained till blast-off.

Sitting on a wall, with a bulging A4 envelope aside me, a smartly dressed lady approached, smiled and lit a cigarette too – one of those long thin ones. Very John le Carré. "Lovely morning," she said. I agreed and budged up so she could perch too. We looked like sunbathing budgerigars. Probably still being overly self-conscious freshly released from prison, I announced that I wasn't casing the joint but was going in there soon, indicating with a flick of my head the Tower. "So am I," she said. Well it is a small world. I suppose it's not uncommon for people to linger outside a venue before an upcoming function.

A Ministry of Justice function at that. Where a full bells and whistles – with all the trimmings – Justice Minister was going to say his piece.

She stuck her non fag-holding hand out and said in the friendliest of ways "I'm Katherine, chief of _____ probation. Who are you?" Shaking her hand, internally voicing *HOLY CRAP*, I told her my name – and then expecting her to depart the scene in *Road-Runner* haste admitted that I was the ex-prisoner with the book-out-any-minute.

She didn't do a runner – but just had another puff on her cigarette before sympathetically omitting "good for you."

Wow. Maybe I'm not going to get carted off to the Tower of London, thought I.

She asked rather wistfully "what's it all about?" A summery of IN IT was volunteered with the voicing of having anticipated either *Shawshank* or *Papillon* (or both) what I in fact got was more a quite artless hack-it to *On the Buses*. And I intended to do something about it. The book would with a bit of luck – put a spoke in the HMP wheel.

Her face momentarily straightened. More than a hint of a sigh was exhaled. "You've got your work cut-out," she guffawed with cryptic pertness. The unsound senseless dredger waste I witnessed was a driving stimulant, I tried to explain. The grim seed of gnawing ambition had been planted by the quagmire more than giving way underfoot on awry-in-prison rehabilitation, I emphasised with almost-pleading-for-support sentiment. The carnage crudeness of it is cringe-worthy, I pleaded.

Risk it for the biscuit, I concluded – so inquired if she would like a copy of one of my press-packs that I had been manufacturing the night before, making my bedroom look like Caxton's laboratory. For this is what my bulging A4 envelope contained. "Oh yes please," she said with more enthusiasm than I had *ever* heard in my dalliance with all matters involving the CJS. She took one, stuffed it in her bag and asked for my details. Name, rank and number was passed, which she fed into one of those electronic tablets. "Come on," she said chucking her ciggie away. "Let's go in."

After non-eventful admission to a conference centre environment and having been given a sticker with my name on it – we all looked like sales-folk at an insurance convention in Slough – the collective were fed and watered. Cups of coffee were held in one hand as suited and booted attendee's nibbled biscuits whilst making polite conversation about the weather, politics and the boy-band One Direction.

I got busy.

The compulsory donning of stickers was *gold dust*. Not only were monikers advertised but so too the names of organisations. Copious representatives from national newspapers were present to hear the Minister speak making them easy meat to identify before having a copy of my press-pack thrust upon them as I post-dropped hither and thither. The scything rampage was such that I ran out – but kept one in reserve. Most satisfying. Soon, the conversation within the space rather dried up as everyone read my bumf. The MoJ personage present on ceremony like fillies at a gymkhana shifted uncomfortably on their feet.

Robinson: 1. MoJ: 0.

One gentleman who got cornered was the Chief Executive of one the countless independent think-tanks that put their heads together on everything from healthcare to motorways – with a bit of prison stuff thrown in. This individual was our host. I had previously emailed him.

He hadn't replied.

On introducing myself – and remarking that he hadn't responded to my email he was pleasant.

But looked uneasy.

Katherine cantered up – smirking post her witnessing of my varmint Fleet Street post-drop. "I don't think I've ever seen an ex-prisoner dishing out press-packs at a *Ministerial* do before. Come on, I'll introduce you to some people," she declared before mother-hen shepherding me to some ladies who more than valiantly represented a Virginia McKenna appreciation society. This lot weren't press – but probation Mafia. Cups and saucers were simultaneously held in three hands by a trio of handbag clad Marks and Spencer's clothing customers of the past (*Ladies* apparel department) as fraternisation with the enemy loomed.

"This is Jonathan. He's an ex-prisoner who has written a book." Three teaspoons on three saucers slightly vibrated and six eyes varnished vapour of stigmatized steaming suspicion towards the trembling author. Katherine was loving it. I could feel her watchfulness.

Robinson: 1. MoJ: 1.

Stand your ground a voice somewhere inside me ordered. Good morning, said I, trying to sound like Grant, Cary but what omitted regretfully resonantly reflected Grant, Russell. Attempt was made to make small talk – which just made the teaspoons vicariously vibrate with more irritation. Residents of Los Angeles would be making for doorways such were the tremors. Still I orally swam against the tide with quivering stifling mundane garbage. The Ice was broken by a fourth member of the *Macbeth* trio joining the scene. A temporary delay of the social viaticum heading my way was made by me reading her name and position from her Paddington Bear label. Just as respite promised rescue, redemption withered as my brain absorbed *who* – and *where* she was from. This lady was another probation chief.

From *my* neck of the woods.

Looking more than bewildered as to why a demonstration of playing-the-spoons was occurring I did what I could only do and said hello, admitting that I was an ex-customer of hers. Flashes of 'is this the man we sold Georgina's pony to?' played across her puzzled face. My suit – and voice – *just* like during my spell in prison, did not give her any inclining that I was an ex-offender – and ex-jailbird for that matter. Her memory was clearly being racked – was this the chap who came round to give a quote on her conservatory roof? To put her out of her misery the record was set straight. Katherine – I think *loving* my discomfort, earned a filthy look from me by telling our new companion that I had written a book about my experience.

The teaspoons hit a crashing cymbal crescendo on that one.

Robinson: 1. MoJ: 2.

"Really? Tell me about it," said this individual who whilst I had been on licence had ultimately controlled the option of sending me back to prison. Over yet more rattle clanking of cutlery I spoon-fed a brief synopsis of what had been written, concluding with a hasty explanation that there was very little reference to her team in the piece and my sights were more centred on the chaos of what happens *in* prison and the complete lack of enthusiasm displayed from insipid management in our jails.

She was thoughtful. "What reference *is* there to my team in your book?" As details of my probation officer often declaring he 'hadn't done this before' and admissions that he 'didn't know what to do next,' were relayed the teaspoons started clanking again. I had to raise my voice a notch or two on my concluding comment that an appointment had been set up for me on the day when everyone was on strike. "Who was your probation officer?"

In prison I had to grass on the officers. Now I'm a probation lawn man. More thought took place. She reached for her teaspoon. Was she was about to join the orchestra?

Instead of producing percussion, the silverware slowly stirred the beverage and I got eyeballed. A good three revolutions were made in the cup before "hmmm" hummed from her.

"I understand what you are trying to do – and you are probably right. The problem is that these sorts of books often cause more damage than good." Just as I was about to open my defence, a Royal Court Theatre bar-bell prefaced an announcement that the performance was about to start.

And indeed a performance it was. The Minister spoke well – but solely focused *only* on our legal system being in the dark ages and announced his intentions to bring the process of court hearings into the 21st century. Non-electronic communication within the system is costing a fortune – and distressing victims of crime. At no time did he mention the mess that is the prison system. Not once. Instead we just heard of the chaos in *Rumpole* land. As he addressed us he was surrounded by posters daubed with 'rehabilitation, less victims and transforming the CJS'.

The elephant in the room – the supersized jumbo jet that everyone knows is an issue but no one has the courage to discuss; our shambolic rehabilitation *in* prison was avoided like the plague.

That is until afterwards.

Have you ever seen a Justice Minister turn green? I have. For yet another soul was jumped on post presentation.

As he was shuffling off-stage I cornered my quarry. The think-tank host tried to parry me but was too late…

"Oh… Erm…. Um… Minister, this is Jonathan Robinson." The Minister stuck his hand out, probably thinking I was part of the clan who had hosted the spectacle. Realising the misidentification the host uttered a supreme Sir Humphrey Appleby explanation. "Jonathan is the ex-prisoner who has written a book."

(Minister's colour changes – handshake goes limp – bushy eyebrows shoot northbound).

As he removed his hand – he had the decency not to check his watch was still there – I gave him my remaining press-pack. Looking like he been handed a live venomous snake he tottered off. He emailed me later:

Many thanks for giving me a copy of the synopsis of your book this morning. If you can let me have a copy of the book, I will read it and share it with the Prisons Minister Jeremy Wright.

Little did he know the named Minister was already armed with said book further to correspondence with the Kingpin of the Kremlin. Apparently, communication within Petty France needs working on too.

BARROWCLOUGH

You're writing a book?

FLETCHER

Yeah – a sort of inside guide to prison life. But don't worry,
I've not overlooked your boys in blue – I will be dealing just as much with your issues as those of our fellow felons.

BARROWCLOUGH

Oh Good. And what are you going to call this book?

FLETCHER

Don't let the bastards grind you down.

Burger Bar Business (Spiggot on a bike)

The Daily Mail 21 February 2013

When robbers snatched £17,000 from a security guard outside a McDonald's, police had a pretty good idea who might have done it. A short distance away, three criminals – including two robbers – were employed on day release from prison.

One was found with more than £5,500 in cash in his pocket and a nearby shed, and refused to say where it came from.

Another matched the description of a one-legged man acting suspiciously in the restaurant.

But extraordinarily, none will face charges because the Crown Prosecution Service says there is insufficient evidence.

Despite this, the money has been confiscated after magistrates decided that, on the balance of probability, it had been taken in the raid.

And the man found with the cash is now on the run after absconding from another open prison.

The astonishing story began when a security guard was collecting takings from the McDonald's in Ipswich on November 7, 2011, and was approached by two able-bodied men.

They shoved her to the ground as they snatched a case she was carrying and ran away.

Within hours Suffolk police had arrested three men.

One was a one-legged man who was shown on CCTV hobbling into the restaurant on crutches. It is understood he later confirmed he had been there – but only to get food.

All three were on a work placement a mile away at Ipswich Town Football Club after being allowed out of Hollesley Bay open prison, near Woodbridge. Police found £5,513 in one of their pockets and at a paint shed at the football ground, to which one held a key.

None of the rest of the stolen cash has been recovered. During a hearing under the Proceeds of Crime Act at South East Suffolk Magistrates' Court, Suffolk police said: 'One man was identified as being a possible suspect and the key being found in his possession that would open the paint store would lend itself [to believing] that the money was involved in that robbery.'

The prosecutor said the case had not met the burden of proof required to bring charges.

She also revealed one of the three had since absconded from another open prison, North Sea Camp in Boston, Lincolnshire.

He has been at large since failing to return from day release on January 23.

He was given six life sentences at the Old Bailey in ____ for carrying out a series of armed robberies at betting shops before escaping on a bicycle.

The Justice Minister (Part Five)

28 February 2013

Just back in work. I will be in touch tomorrow.

Thanks

Red Letter Day (Part Twenty)

28 February 2013

Dear Johnathan,

Thank you for your recent letter, I tend to pay more attention to your words of wisdom than others, I just wish I payed attention 10 months ago when it would have saved me.

My future is most important as is my sanity and I am loosing both at the moment! My landlord is having kittens about how long its been and its on the skin of my teeth im holding on to my release address.

I am counting on your continued support. you are a voice of reason and sanity in my life and probably the only person I listen to.

I am still waiting for my PB asnerw from the 8th Feb its now 27 and they said 2 weeks max so im well over? If I don't get it I will loose my flat and then it will create problems with probation! I must get out and on my feet with work and stuff.

Every time I hear keys I think there coming to tell me to pack and leave! its doing my head in. im sorry its all me me me! But my head is up my arse with anxiiety, this is getting the better of me now. I need out!

I am honerd for your support and take your guidance very seriously indeed. I concure you are 100% right!!!

Speak soon mate   Your friend Rod

The Boot

By way of banging the drum as take-off for IN IT neared a *very* well-known public figurehead was emailed in attempt to get her – for it's a she – on board the soon to depart wobbly flight that is prison reform. The communiqué was kept short and sweet – alerting her of what I was up to and requesting permission for my volume to be given the once-over. The two or three paragraphs deliberately contained snippets of typical JR schoolboy humour. That'll crack *her*, I thought.

Wrong.

With the sent box still pulsating my phone rang, displaying a restricted number. A more than familiar voice asked to speak to me. Conker bearing satchel equipped Latin book wheedling Terry Scott prep-school thanks were bleated down the phone assuming this strategy was going to pay off. I nearly asked if she wanted to see my marble collection.

When will I *ever* learn?

It sort of *started* ok. She said something like "how can I help?" Assuming the somewhat tongue-in-cheek approach had cracked the nut, the ploy continued. Verbal affirmation was transmitted with more than behind-the-bike shed method of the bare-bones of my piece and she was asked directly if I could ferry it to her – in hindsight; with probably too much playground schmoozing. There was one of those silent moments – and a Mistral taking-in of breath at the other end of the phone before: "I don't have time to read it, Mr Robinson."

The road was too far taken to change direction – there could be no tactical turning back – so a final detention avoiding push was made to break the iceberg. Flying by the seat of my pants – shooting from the hip – out came: Oh please do, it's a great cure for insomnia.

Before the call was *firmly* terminated I got:

"I don't SUFFER from insomnia Mr Robinson. *GOODBYE.*" (Click).

I bet she wasn't like that with Morecambe and Wise.

You are not going to the Ball

As well as appeals to Academy Award winners past to read the forthcoming 'book what I wrote' *Inside Time*, the lifeline prisoner newspaper had been given a heads-up on the nearing launch of IN IT. They were to become a huge ally. Their Managing Editor – who incidentally is an exact double of the late David Lean – dropped message to me forewarning the nervous-soon-to-be-published author of another Ministerial do.

Ironically, slated for the day before blast-off of the book.

This was a *big* one – for both Mr Grayling and Mr Wright – the two names-above-the-titles Ministers, had their names above the titles. Both were attending – and both would be speaking.

The press-pack production department got busy again chez JR.

Playing by the rules, an email was despatched to my man at the Ministry asking if I could attend:

Before you telephone me this afternoon please can you put me on the list to attend this, which *Inside Time* has sent on to me.

I will BEHAVE.

Jonathan.

Which he responded with thus:

Hi,

Unfortunately this is not an MoJ event, so I can't really put your name on the list. It's probably best to drop them an email, and ask them directly.

I rang the organisers – making it *crystal* clear I was an ex-prisoner – asking to attend and shortly received this:

We are delighted that you have registered to attend our full day conference, *Delivering the Rehabilitation Revolution*, on Monday 4th March. We look forward to seeing you on Monday. Kind regards

Again playing by the rules, to keep Ministry Man in the loop, this was sent:

Hi____,

I'd already used my initiative (not encouraged in prisons) and have emailed them and have been confirmed. I promise you I will behave and undertake:

Not to start any tunnels.
Not to read newspapers during the event like some people do when they are at work.
Not to go to sleep like some people do when they are at work.
Not to visit any burger bars at lunchtime (on one leg).
To show interest and passion in the many problems facing the HMP/rehabilitation event. I fear I will be the minority.

I understand you will be calling me later with initial MoJ reaction to IN IT. I look forward to hearing from you and to setting up promised meeting.

Best,

Jonathan.

Assuming my Willy Wonka Golden Ticket was secure, *Inside Time* was alerted that I would be there and so started thinking about which shirt to iron. Meanwhile my printer was chugging-out more press-packs, the plan being to use this gathering as an opportunity to dish out information on the book – and to let those present in on what is *really* – not – happening in our jails. I at no time even considered loading my pockets with rotten fruit – or heckling. Despite making a Minister change colour at the last event that I had attended I had – in my opinion – behaved in an exemplary manner and not chinned anyone. Besides, what would be the point of making trouble? It never crossed my mind. Stealth and JR tongue-in-cheek was the game plan.

Meanwhile, some frantic Jim Hacker/Bernard Woolley telephone calls were going on behind the scenes. I can only imagine various alarm bells were ringing off the walls and someone uttering *"you've done what? You said HE could come? Are you out of your MIND? He's the one that dishes out press-packs for Chrissake"*. For it wasn't long before I received this in full spurious grandeur:

Dear Jonathan,

Many thanks for your phone call to _____ earlier today.

We have been inundated with requests for places at this event, which _____ was unaware of. I have a waiting list with 30 names on it, and should space become available they will have first priority. As such, I am unable to offer you a place at Monday's event.

The event will be filmed and the footage will be available on our YouTube channel shortly after the event.

Kindest Regards,

———

Head of Events

Ever felt you've been had? Smelling a rat – a gargantuan *king* rat – an email was fired at the Ministry. Their reply:

That's annoying. I do know this event is incredibly busy. It is difficult for me to intervene though. Apologies.

I am going to struggle to call you this afternoon, but are you available on Monday lunchtime for me to call? In terms of a meeting, perhaps March 15th works for you?

Fuming at the system's fobbing off – are they so afraid of the truth? – realisation set in that I was not going to the ball and had been well and truly sent to Coventry. I just so wish that someone had possessed balls enough to admit my presence simply wasn't welcome. This was a key moment in understanding how the management of clink are incapable of admitting that the king has no clothes on.

Mentor Offenders

The Daily Telegraph

4 March 2013

Jeremy Wright, the Prisons Minister, said "Peer mentoring is going on inside prisons. It seems to work extremely effectively".

5 March

All sorts of things happened on 5/3/13. The first groundbreaker of the day in the Robinson household was receipt of an email from *Inside Time* – which didn't *really* surprise me:

Jonathan just to report that loads of seats were empty at the Ministerial do yesterday.

Very best

As well as this earth shattering news it was my wedding anniversary.

Oh – and a book came out too.

All those days and nights in prison where whenever I would feel blue, shame or panic – I would focus my mind on the book. Maybe one day it would actually get out into the big wide world. And so it came that on March 5th, 2013, IN IT did exactly that. I felt a complete fraud. Me a *writer*? Ha.

Little did I know that on the evening of blast-off, a very valid conversation was taking place on the subject of mentoring, the in-house, in-prison activity that is recognised as a proven commodity in the battle of reducing reoffending.

The in-house shooting down of this in an open resettlement prison – via teaching illiterate adult prisoners to *read* – was now in the public domain. The battle lines had been drawn.

The Prison Reform Trust (Part Two)

5 March 2013

Committee Room 6, House of Commons Mentoring Offenders

I have been a volunteer mentor for nearly three years now. I am also an ex-offender. This is a costly and time consuming process but the personal satisfaction I gain from helping the guys makes it all worthwhile.

Why did I want to become a mentor? During the time I spent in prison I saw the need to help guys who were in desperate need of a helping hand to keep them on the straight and narrow when they got out of prison. They need to have someone they can look up to, and hopefully with guidance make a fresh start.

I also saw untapped talents, skills and desire, sadly so often suppressed, and the true hope to get free of the reoffending cycle. Many cannot, but want to start a new life; they need someone to give them moral and practical support as they step out of prison life and into the daunting world of freedom. From my experience, the first few weeks of freedom can be very challenging, especially if they have no accommodation, no family or friends to help, and often nothing but the tee-shirt and pair of jeans they stand in.

I care about wanting to help people aspire to a fresh start in their lives. I believe that time and investment in helping guys when they first get out is the best possible chance they have of not drifting back to prison again. Luckily for me, when I went to prison I had the support of a loving family and close friends to help. The vast majority of people getting out of prison do not have this. The lure of old habits and bad influences are very strong. I was also fortunate to get into full time work and sustain employment as an ex offender. It is a passion of mine to guide my clients in the right direction to work and a better quality of life.

I helped one 17 year old client recently, with a history of crime and behavioural problems, to recognise his talents in fixing motor bikes and cars. We went to the local college where he took his test to see if he could get a mechanics apprenticeship. Not only did he get top marks, he got the apprenticeship with a local garage and is now fully entrenched in full time work. No longer does he steal motor bikes and cars, he fixes them. His pride and belief in himself is back, his girlfriend and her family are so proud and he earning an honest crust for the first time. This is fantastic; this is mentoring at its best.

Our role can often be the vital cog in the wheel and only with mentor engagement can we begin to break the cycle of reoffending. It is my hope that law abiding citizens not only understand the benefits of true rehabilitation of the ex-offender, but that they also see we are not 'goody two shoes', making excuses for the criminal. Of course punishment for wrong-doing is necessary; it was right that I was punished. But how much better society would be if we reduced reoffending and the need for sending people to prison by giving them hope and self-belief. This for me is mentoring in action. The vision of genuine rehabilitation lies in helping people like me, a reformed ex-offender, and hopefully many more people from all backgrounds who I hope will be encouraged to go into mentoring.

Ministry of Justice Spokeswoman

On the day IN IT was published, one newspaper that covered the launch contacted the Ministry of Justice for a comment. What they got was: *"The government remains committed to making prisons places of hard work and activity giving offenders the opportunity to turn away from crime and live purposeful and productive lives."*

That quote was framed and now hangs in my lavatory.

IN IT Flashback (Part Two)

Work. Dave on duty. All very quiet. Do the loos and vacuum Rachel's office, which has been painted and a huge parachute sized dust sheet covers her desk and computer. Dave and I discuss the inactivity. I tell him it's because everyone is still in bed. He seems close to despair.

HMP Hollesley Bay Staff Member

Hi

Before we start 2 reasons why I did not reply to your first e-mail (in way of an apology). Firstly I felt that you needed to get a bit of distance to give you some perspective (my call) secondly and more importantly I felt that the powers that "be" would frown upon contact. (May still, but feeling a bit braver now).

Well done, both on the book and the article in the paper, I saw the article and downloaded the book and have read it. Have laughed a lot and found your insight into prison life enlightening. I would love to tell you more about how things are but I suspect that would be frowned upon even more!!!! I have discussed the article and the book at work so feel sure that the word will out!

I hope that life has moved on for you, oddly enough I often think of you when a helicopter flies overhead, I do hope that you have returned to the sky where you clearly feel at home.

Lastly, I do hope she has read it if nothing else the book stands as both an apology and an appeal from the heart.

Good luck once again

The Bedford MP

During one of the now regular phone calls with my MP's office his assistant had a brainwave. "You should get in touch with Bedford's MP and shake some branches there." The fact that I was not a Bedford constituent – any more – was aired. "Doesn't matter. The prison's on his patch. I'll send you his details. He's one of your lot – but he's sensible."

Yet again I repeat how marvellous my Member of Parliament – and his clan – have been. I think it was around this time that I learnt that he – and other notable shakers and stirrers introduced to me via this valuable ally, had paid a visit to HMP Bedford following various meetings with me – wanting to see for themselves the 'rehabilitation' going on.

One dignitary reported back to me following this snooping that 'the place was a dustbin'.

I need at this point to make something VERY clear. Neither IN IT nor what you are reading now (what, you're still here?) is in ANY way a whinge that the quality of wallpaper in our prisons isn't up to scratch. I have no qualms at *all* with prisons being ghastly places – what I do however have *major* issues with is the third-rate so-called 'rehabilitation' taking place. It is gritless.

From experience, the preferred colour of prison-issue clothing is Burgundy. If you stick a bottle of Burgundy somewhere and *do nothing with it* – it will eventually turn to vinegar. Redundant Palaeontologists kicking their heels could do well with studying the fossil philosophy of rehabilitation in our jails.

Both originate from the same Jurassic era.

Getting off the phone from my assistant, sorry, my MP's assistant, an email popped up with the details for Bedford's Member of Parliament. Communication was sent – briefly outlining my story and what I was up to. The upcoming meeting with MoJ militia was revealed and a request for an audience was passed.

I got a reply that evening:

Jonathan

Would be good to meet, and might make sense to do so AFTER your MoJ meeting. Would Bedford or London be better for you?

Next week in London I could do times on Monday afternoon or Wednesday or Thursday mornings.

If Bedford, I could do this Saturday (16th) in the afternoon

Best wishes

Penned Politician Prisoner Penning

March 2013

Dear Mr Huhne,

I *hope* this finds its way to you…

We have never met (don't panic!) but I wanted to write to you because I am an ex-prisoner (July 25th, 2011 – November 21st, 2011) and give you some support. I was an idiot who stole some money from my employers and got all that I had coming to me. I still don't think 17 weeks in stir long enough a punishment for me but there we go…

Whilst not a politician but certainly an ex-public school boy I was *terrified* of the prospect of Lord knows what coming my way in prison… BOY WAS I WRONG. Instead of being used for target practice I found a community of classless camaraderie who (even with the odd taking the ***** out of me) without doubt *all* helped me through the slog. There are some people in prison who have great potential and marvellous humour (look what Dick Clement and Ian La Frenais did) and once you have found your feet, I guarantee you will look back one day at your experience and chuckle. I tried to use prison as the making of me, not the breaking of me. I am sure you will manage to do the same.

Stay strong. Keep your head up and one day it'll all be over. Best wishes to you.

Jonathan Robinson

The Bedford MP (Part Two)

12 March 2013

Having written to a jailed MP in the morning Bedford jail's MP emailed me shortly afterwards:

Great. Let's meet at 2pm on Saturday 16th at my office. See you there then

I responded thanking him for the appointment and started mental preparation for my forthcoming MoJ meeting with the suits three days hence. This was going to be vital. Thoughts crossed my mind that my light touch – the comedy mannerisms in the book – may not have gone down too well but if the humour had opened another front on the prison problem – then I had made a small chink on clink. Besides, I suppose they had to listen – even if it was lip-service – as lots of people were (thank God) actually spending their hard earned cash on my log of please-laugh-and-weep prison sentence past. Enough for it to hit the charts… Enough for the Bedford MP to email me again that day…

IN IT has charted at number 19, just ahead of Chavs and just behind Al Gore... go figure!

It Weren't Us, Gov'nor (Part Two)

14 March 2013

The day before my meeting with the MoJ, the following email was received from the company that provides education services at HMP Hollesley Bay:

Jonathan,

Thanks for sending your note through. I forwarded it on to a number of colleagues with an interest in this area.

As ever, best of luck with the release.

Attempting to sort out the barring of peer-mentoring – *teaching prisoners to read* – and somehow stopping it ever *happening again* I replied thus:

Smashing – thanks.

I am meeting MoJ personage tomorrow (15th) and suggest one of your lot give me a buzz next week?

Best, Jonathan.

Now Pay Attention 007

March 2013

Jonathan

If the opportunity arises do mention that Shannon Trust has the potential to be a significant source for the thousands of experienced mentors he needs for his through the gate project. We train some 1,700 mentors per year. This can be significantly increased but we would only do so if we are able to match them with learners. We have learnt from hard experience that there is nothing more frustrating for a prisoner to be trained as a mentor and then not give them someone to mentor.

The Justice Minister (Part Six)

March 2013

There's a cafe opposite Big Ben. The sort of place where in the good old days Albert Finney could be snapped in black and white reading a bed-sheet sized *Daily Express* smoking a cigarette drinking a cup of tea. Those days when a cuppa cost less than a newspaper. I floundered in a corner surrounded by people who didn't speak English – some of them were tourists – and sipped a cappuccino from a paper cup.

When a film maker wishes to indicate plot of significance is heading the audience's way from the heart of London, more often than not Big Ben is depicted. I studied the opal glass and pondered my forthcoming meeting.

With the Ministry of Justice.

The heavy mob.

The management.

During my time in prison I would invariably lie awake in bed at night wondering if the acres of words I was writing – my pen and I inseparable – would ever see the light of day. Now I was out of prison, IN IT had been out exactly ten days, the gentlemen from the Ministry had read it and requested the pleasure of my company. Progress.

Now was my chance to get something done.

Coffee finished, I stood up and left. The walk to Portcullis House five minutes. My second visit. Now a dab-hand at the security formality of entrance – fully accustomed, I sat and waited.

Nervously.

He appeared bang on time – dressed as a prep school geography teacher – having walked from the MoJ bunker in Petty France. When we'd spoken on the phone to pinpoint the location for our meeting I had suggested coming straight to their HQ. This notion had been met like I'd offered to bring Ronnie Biggs with me. He'd started talking about a coffee bar – conveniently *miles* from the gazes of people with consequence. When he learnt that I was familiar with the glittering aluminium bronze arches that support the inside of the Bridge Street building he relented the Cornish granite stance of allowing me anywhere near where-it-all-happens – and where for *each* MP there is a reclining chair that cost a trifling £440 – so here we were squaring up, judging one another's measure.

He was friendly. And polite.

He'd stood as a candidate for the Conservative party in a parliamentary constituency election in 2010 and come a close second. In 2012 he had left his post as the Chief Operating officer of a social reform business to become Special Advisor to Chris Grayling the Minister of Justice.

He did not have a firm handshake.

But he did have one of those *Mr Bean* leather purses and he rummaged around inside it for some change as he bought us both a cup of coffee. We sat down. He kicked-off with a straightforward question. "Jonathan, why doesn't prison work?"

For the next twenty minutes or so I blunderbuss blabbed condiments of nondescript prison officers asleep on duty, the metronomic erosion wretched wasted opportunity of rehabilitating people whilst they are *in* prison, the hope that my book might actually make his lot twig that they acutely need to fuse retribution and rehabilitation *together* and the complete lack of morale and leadership from the majority of most of the staff – any bygone *Porridge* enthusiasm is now charred to a cinder. 'Glenda' of HMP Bedford's library was praised to the skies and should, I recommended, be put in charge of the whole shooting-match by tea time. The realisation of the abhorrent lack of motivation – from experience, contagious among *anyone* involved in the system – and how that surplus of total lack of innovation inspired – *impelled* me – to grab a pen, was declared to the best of my ability. Hand on heart. I wrapped with law and order is needed in prison. It ain't there now.

I'm not sure he got that.

Or perhaps he was more implicitly inclined to ignore it. That's a surprise, isn't it?

Instead, he made the odd glib remark that this or that in the book was funny. He specifically wanted peremptory information on the telly channels available on E wing at Bedford. When verbal confirmation was testified that the girlie channels were available – as logged within the book – my host's eyebrows joined the bronze on the ceiling.

During the conversation he kept saying "Chris is keen on doing that" and "Chris is most interested in doing this." It was all Chris this and Chris that. I kept referring to him as Mr Grayling or the Justice Minister. Etiquette and all that. By the end though, I too was referencing the Dark Knight as 'Chris'.

If you can't beat 'em join 'em. Mixing it with the big boys.

Throughout the – friendly – interrogation, all of his questions were answered openly and honestly. There was a *lot* of eye rolling and head shaking. After yet more conversation of the system missing a trick on remolding people whilst they are *in* custody I somehow veered the conversation to events of September 1st, 2011, when Toe by Toe had been – unaccountably – barred in an open resettlement prison by the Head of Education of a private education provider that 'Chris' was chucking more than seven and a half million pounds at. His reply – in my naivety – made my whole body stiffen.

"We cannot comment on a specific incident."

What?

He – being a politician – without moving one muscle in his face, without a hint of eyelid activity, economically changed the subject. He skirted it – with ingenious brazen flawless flourish. A shrank sidestep in a minefield. Political chicanery up close and personal.

Perplexed, I could not utter a word. Recovering, attempt without preamble was rakishly made – with febrile feistiness – to dig deeper by getting the discussion back to where I wanted it. That failed. Dismally. He resolutely had other ideas. The closest I got to wooing him back-on track induced a sudden dazzling flicker of recognition on his impassive bleak face before he steadfastly shied incongruously away with "I am not going to attack this government."

Call me daft – call me whatever you like – this utterly ursine aloofness caused me stupefaction. A quote from the Prime Minister a few months before this meeting, as pretty as irony: *"In prison there are people who cannot read. These people need help. It's common sense."*

The last time I looked, our Dave is the boss. The General. Thinking along those lines Chris is Captain Mainwaring making Sergeant Wilson here – supposedly – part of the chain of command. Why the *evasiveness* about Hollesley Bay's Hodges? Why was he *so* reluctant to admit things were not as they should be, to so defiantly – with perspicacity – *ignore* this with such soldierly obtuseness?

I sound like Andy Dufresne.

This tall drink of water with the silver spoon up his ass learnt right then that politicians are quantifiably incapable of holding their hands up after the reins have been dropped by acknowledging mistakes. Especially on the insubstantial pitiable *prison issue*. The benevolence best I got out of him was that there was indeed occasional reference at the Ministry of Justice concerning the 'September the first incident'.

My head was swimming. This was hopeless.

Bugger up life. Get sent to prison. Official ignominy disgrace – but – get hit with *nuclear fall-out* realisation why prison fails. Write book about it. Release book. Get asked by MoJ management for book. Get summoned for meeting by MoJ mob. Attend said meeting assuming they would fix this…

Wrong.

Swirling vortex waffle followed. Anything else I uttered was desolation guesswork. My brain was full of cotton wool. I had got this far. So close…but *no* cigar. His parting words to me were short shrift assurances that he'd be in touch. Oh – he also urbanely asked me if it was possible if I could reduce the amount of drum-banging towards the press as it was 'embarrassing' as the MoJ press office were piqued and kept asking him 'what's going on,' he said with a bitter chagrin.

On the way home – having left as I arrived – nowhere – my mind whirred. *Brubaker* – the 1980 Robert Redford prison reform film – was considered and character Lillian Gray's integral line:

"You can't reform the system if you're not in it…"

In it? I was now *on it*. Hard on it – hardened to resolve the farce. I knew what I had to do. It was quite clear. Acceptance kicked-in that I was politically hopelessly inadequate for the job – but the knives were drawn.

The Bedford MP (Part Three)

March 2013

He arrived most punctually. Bit of a scraggy suit. A friendly welcome though. A slight twang in accent indicated time spent the other side of the pond. His office – for surgeries with his constituents – could easily have been a lettings agency. After shaking my hand a chair was motioned to. We got stuck in.

He listened to my fables like I imagine a brittle University Don would audition a potential new student. No tobacco pouch to play with as thoughtful filling of pipe occurred though. Instead he obliquely tinkered with his iPhone. I explained my primary focus was the fact that I had been barred from tutoring Toe by Toe – in an open prison – by a company getting more than a hefty amount of pound notes from the paymasters of government. The iPhone tampering ceased on that. Geographical location of that in-house cessation of common-sense was pointed at – thus not on his patch. What *was* on his watch though was HMP Bedford and staff found asleep on duty – in the prison I now knew to top the suicide tables, enough drugs to make a heavy-metal band put their guitars down and despite Bedford being a hub-prison, the theory of so-called rehabilitation is kicked into touch as soon as the referee blows his whistle for the action to commence.

The iPhone was put down and a quizzical look made.

The procedures of landing in prison were passed – and the paperwork practice of 'Induction' revealed. This is the first pamphlet the 'system' proffers prisoners on the road to 'rehabilitation' and it is stuffed with spelling mistakes and grammatical errors.

The iPhone was not played with for the rest of the meeting. Not a lot else of resonance was said.

Above all else, the impression I came away with was that he – and the rest of the malevolant mélange of *suits* – are not terribly *interested* in prison issues. If anything, an ingenious lusty capacity for avoiding the issue – apparently obligatory – is the raison d'être of Westminster. Prison policy, is a *vestive* of interest *long* departed. If you're a noble politician – and you hear 'jail' – turn tail *now* with hair-trigger twitchiness…

All outgoing mail must include your name, prison number and full prison address.

You may write your letters in the language of their choice, but any letters subject to reading will be translated which could caus a delay to your mail leaving the establishment.

Mail will be read if :

It Weren't Us, Gov'nor (Part Three)

21 March 2013

Despite having asked for a phone call from someone with passion/interest/gumption from those who manage education at my ex-prison my phone hadn't squeaked at all. A stony silence. Well nothing from their direction.

Feedback from others had been more than forthcoming, most expressing outrage and disbelief of September 1st events at the Bay.

A wake-up prod was poked via email…

Hi ____,

Trust you are well.

I met with MoJ personage last Friday.

You would not BELIEVE the comments that I have had back reference September 1st from peeps who have read IN IT. They include current staff at Hollesley Bay, probation staff, ex-offenders, MP's, members of the public.... the list goes on and on...

As previously communicated it is most clear that ____ does have some people within it with passion, I detected that from you when we met. However I am NOT going to let this go until something is done.

Can I please urge someone (with clout) from your lot to get in touch with me.

I repeat again that I am not being bloody minded – I just want prison – and all that occurs within it – to make sense.

Best – and sorry to use you as a post box!

Jonathan.

Sir Sean Connery

"My first big break came when I was five years old. It's taken me more than seventy years to realise that. You see, at five I first learnt to read. It's that simple and it's that profound."

It Weren't Us, Gov'nor (Part Four)

23 March 2013

Hi Jonathan,

Firstly, thank you for sending on an excerpt from your book relating to 1st September 2011 at HMP Hollesley Bay.

As I explained in my email of 11th February, the most appropriate way for us to deal with this matter, and to investigate the events in question, is for you to follow our complaints procedure. To do this, you will need to outline the exact cause/nature of your dissatisfaction with _____ specifically (rather than with staff employed by HMPS or other non-___ staff working at HMP Hollesley Bay).

To follow this process, you can contact our Customer Service team directly, either by letter, telephone or email. There is more information on our website (www._____) but I can help you with their contact details:

Telephone 0800 _____ Email: _____
Post: Customer Services
____
_____ _____
_____ _____
_____
_____

Best wishes

Prison Service Orders (Part Eleven)

Order Number 4190

Strategy for Working with the Voluntary and Community Sector

Responsibility at Senior Level in establishments: Mandatory Action:

Governors, Area Managers and Head of Groups must:

Ensure that the understanding and trust needed for working in partnership is created and that staff understand: why voluntary groups have been invited to work in the prison, what they do and how this benefits the prison, themselves as staff, and prisoners.

It Weren't Us, Gov'nor (Part Five)

23 March 2013

Hi _____,

Good to hear from you – on a Saturday and in the snow too!

One of the crucial purposes of IN IT is to display that the bean-feast of bureaucratic form-filling is not the answer to rehabilitation in prison but passion is. Now that you are aware of the unfathomable events that took place – although I gave you a very clear heads-up when we met in February (before publication of IN IT) that an individual within your ranks perhaps doesn't make your organisation look terribly chipper, I am somewhat astonished that you are inviting me to fill in a form.

At my recent MoJ meeting the internal squabbling between in-house prison agencies was raised. I didn't flag it, the MoJ did. The reason why non staff got involved is because YOUR REPRESENTATIVE told me to "Go back to Tribal" (Sic).

Since publication of IN IT, all feedback received from politicians, probation staff, ex-offenders, the press and the public has been overwhelmingly positive. Alarmingly, the individuals who have got in touch with me from HMP Hollesley Bay – *who work there* – have proclaimed that I have 'nailed it'.

These people are at the coalface. And you're asking me to fill in *forms*?

A quote from your website:

"We believe that every prisoner or offender should be engaged in work-focused activities."

I am afraid actions by the Head of Education during September 2011 at HMP Hollesley Bay heavily contradict this. Everyone is of the opinion that schemes like Toe by Toe only do good – I find the shooting-down of it inexcusable.

In May of 2012, the then Employment Minister Chris Grayling dispensed ____'s services because 'continuing would be too great a risk'. At my recent MoJ meeting, it was made VERY clear to me that personage from the Ministry 'couldn't comment on specific incidents' so it appears that the sorting out of this mess is down to me.

Let me be very clear with you. No one is perfect – Jeez, look at the pathetic behaviour of mine that resulted with me being thrown into prison. However, what I witnessed and experienced has made me determined to see that things like this never happen again. I have no wish for any cessation of ___'s involvement in clink. Clearly there are people within the group with passion – the weekend timing of your email today is prima facie of that. However, the 'complaints procedure' that you have asked me to commence is not going to happen. Instead I pleadingly positively URGE someone from ___ (with clout) to get in touch with me, acknowledge that things were not handled correctly (I am being VERY polite and reasonable here) and then publically announce that errors were made and most VITALLY, that they will not reoccur.

If _____ needs something in writing – read IN IT.

I do so hope to hear from someone soon. Meanwhile, I ain't gonna stop. With best regards,

Jonathan.

NICHOLSON

Hughes, if this was your bridge, how would you use the men?

HUGHES

Well Sir, not the way they're doing it. It's utter chaos – as you can see at a glance. A lot of uncoordinated activity. No teamwork. Some of those parties are actually working against each other.

NICHOLSON

I tell you gentlemen, we have a problem on our hands.

The Prison Ombudsman

2 April 2013

Dear Sirs,

I am an ex-prisoner, sentenced (quite rightly) for 15 months (probably *not* enough) for theft on July 25th 2011 and served my time (17 weeks or so) at HMP Bedford and HMP Hollesley Bay.

During which a book was written which came out on March 5th of this year. I am NOT writing to you in order to promote my piece.

However, I am writing to you in connection to an event that took place on September 1st, 2011 which I attempted to resolve whilst still in prison and have tried my best to get sorted with individuals post meeting representatives from a certain company at a function on prison reform hosted by _____ MP. This has got me <u>nowhere</u> and thus am finally contacting yourselves.

I hope you can help me and more importantly, I hope any findings you make will ensure that events like that which took place will *never happen again.*

To make your life easier at the foot of this letter is that day's entry within my book which will give you a taster of what my issue is. Subsequent days in prison were spent trying to resolve the issue – with no luck. I am somewhat flummoxed (still) by events and even more so by the reaction from a certain in-prison-education provider.

I enclose too copy of correspondence to Chris Grayling (which he responded to in 55 minutes). I had my first meeting with MOJ personage on March 15th. I also enclose copies of emails between a certain education company and me.

I really do hope you can help me.

The Open Prison MP

18 April 2013

Having been prodded by my MP's office to contact HMP Bedford's political ring-master It was agreed that getting in touch with Hollesley Bay's tightrope walker was a good idea and that (she) should be alerted that rehabilitation had been sunk from within at her local open – resettlement – prison.

Various emails were transmitted. Not a lot of interest was shown. Until I received this:

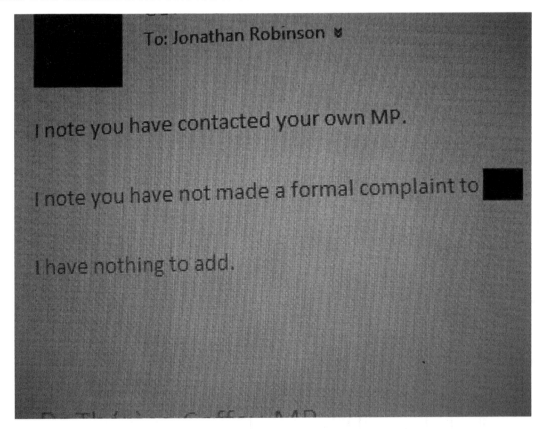

My MP chuckled when this was forwarded to his office. His staff told me that they would 'never ever – *ever* – reply to an email like that – to *anyone.*'

Good this prison reform stuff isn't it?

Well, if it was easy I suppose everyone would be doing it.

Penned Politician Prisoner Penning (Part Two)

I interpreted about 5% of the following. Anyone who can beat that please get in touch! I *think* he was pleased to hear from me and I *think* he agrees with me but who knows?

It Weren't Us, Gov'nor (Part Six)

28 March 2013

Jonathan,

I'm sorry that you feel ____ prevented you from helping other people to read.

We have taken the time to look into the events in question in more detail and can find no evidence to support your claim that _____, specifically, prevented you from helping another learner to read.

In the information you have circulated, you make a series of allegations about events at HMP Hollesley Bay which incorrectly attribute ____ members of staff as being involved. Using only this extract, it is very difficult to ascertain exactly which staff member(s) you refer to through these exchanges, but it appears that you have incorrectly identified a number of people as being employed by ___, and we believe these individuals are/were employed by Tribal, LearnDirect, and HM Prison Service.

You correctly reference that ___ supports the view that 'every prisoner should be engaged in work-focused activities'. We have actively supported the transformation of prison education to have a greater focus on employment and skills, and wherever possible, we look to support practical learning opportunities.

You have accused ____'s Head of Education of 'shooting down' Toe-by-Toe. However, it is not accurate to report that in this instance, ___ prevented you from being employed as a peer mentor.

To reiterate, I'm afraid that your suggestion that ____ prevented you from working in the capacity you had desired is inaccurate.

IN IT Flashback (Part Three)

"Come and meet the *Head of Education*." I followed her into a small back office where the *holder of this title* lived...

He asked me to bring him up to date with the morning's events... I gave him the whole shooting match in detail...

"The person who told you to do Toe By Toe has no power in this prison..."

I am to *"Scrub the Monday appointment..."*

"There will be no Toe by Toe in this prison."

J K Rowling

"Learning to read represents a significant turning point in anyone's life, and may be the one thing that makes a difference to help people in prison turn their lives around."

Education Provider's Website

Work In Prisons

"As many as 80% of prisoners have a reading age below that of an eleven year old. That's why we're so committed to helping thousands of offenders develop skills and qualifications while in prison."

Prison Service Orders (Part Twelve)

Order Number 4190

Strategy for Working with the Voluntary and Community Sector

Responsibility at Senior Level in establishments: Mandatory Action: Governors, Area Managers and Head of Groups must: Take action against anyone who is found to discriminate unfairly against voluntary and community sector staff or volunteers working in the establishment.

It Weren't Us, Gov'nor (Part Seven)

28 March 2013

Hi ____,

I only ever seem to hear from you on – or near weekends.

The gentleman who barred me from teaching prisoners to read at HMP Hollesley Bay on September 1, 2011 was a Mr _____ who is VERY CLEARLY an employee of __ as per your website:

    "_____ _____ Education Manager at Hollesley Bay." www._____

The actions of Mr _____ contradict everything that your website claims that _____ do.

I have learnt that your in-prison-education contract earns ___ £7,751,340,00 during 2012/2013.

I set up appointments with a prisoner (in order to *teach him to read*) and Mr _____ *ordered me to cancel them*. See Book. See also in said book subsequent pleas from me to 'Frank' to sort this, whom Mr _____ referred me to after barring me from TEACHING PRISONERS TO READ IN MY OWN TIME IN AN OPEN PRISON.

After your email of last weekend inviting me to fill in forms and your email of today denying that _____ stopped me from teaching prisoners to read I am totally dumbfounded.

If – once you have re checked all the above – you come back to me and admit mistakes were made (by _____) and they will never happen again, then we can all move forward.

Until then – my campaign continues.

As per my email of last weekend I urge you to get someone (with clout) from _____ to get in touch with me. I found the actions of Mr_____ inexcusable and am doing my best to stop shambolic events like these ever happening in a prison again. Once things start making sense maybe the system might start having some success...

Happy Easter!

Jonathan.

(Author: This email was never replied to. To this day I have heard *nothing* further – at all – from the company that runs education at HMP Hollesley Bay).

VON LUGER

Are all flying officers so ill-mannered?

HILTS

Yeah, about 99 percent.

VON LUGER

Then perhaps while you are here with us you will have a chance to learn some. Ten days isolation, Hilts.

HILTS

Captain Hilts.

VON LUGER

Twenty days.

HILTS

Right. Oh, uh, you'll still be here when I get out?

VON LUGER

[visibly annoyed] *Cooler!*

The Prime Minister (Part Two)

"Almost 70% of prisoners are illiterate. The Shannon Trust's Toe by Toe, in which prisoners are trained to teach other prisoners to read has a remarkable success rate and deals with one of the most profound problems in our prisons. Sitting in a room with 40 inmates, some of whom are now fully trained mentors and others well on their way to reading and writing properly, is an inspiring experience. There were no teachers there to explain how they had transformed anyone's life chances – it was prisoners themselves doing the talking about their work, with all the benefits for self-esteem that follows."

Prison Service Orders (Part Thirteen)

Order Number 2300 Resettlement

Activities and programmes such as education, training and prison work must be coordinated for resettlement purposes, with the ultimate aim of reducing reoffending. Work to improve prisoners' skills must focus on increasing the likelihood of their gaining employment on release.

The Prison Reform Trust (Part Three)

April 2013

National Chairman, Prison Officers Association: Employers want somebody who is now safe, and who is literate. That is something we should be able to provide. There is no point in just throwing somebody into a workshop environment with these issues. Work has got to run alongside the education services.

The CAA (Part Two)

11 April 2013

Outbound

Hello _____,

I have left a number of messages for you and have not heard back from you. Please can you give me a ring!

Jonathan.

Inbound

Jonathan

I'm in meetings most of the day – like every day really! What is it you are asking for? It is better that we write to one another, that way correspondence between us can be retained on your file.

In responding, please include '_____._____@caa.co.uk' as a matter of routine. With thanks,

Best regards

Outbound

Just wanted an update/judgement on our meeting! I have not heard anything from you since! _____ _____ MP told me that you wrote to him – and that's all I know… I am trying to work out what to do.

Best,

Jonathan.

Inbound

We wrote to _____ and _____ on 21 December 2012 for references and to date only____ _____ has replied to our letter.

Regards

Thank you for the update. _____ MP's email address is C/O _____ _____@parliament.uk. FYI a link to his blog within which he talks of me is www._____

I suppose the fact that an MP is happy to mention me is some form of reference!

I have also had a meeting with Chris Grayling's right-hand-man:
_____._____@justice.gsi.gov.uk

I wonder if the Authority could give me some sort of indication if it is happy for me to renew my instructor's certificate. My hand is now back to 100% since pre-Xmas surgery and I would like to be in a position to earn some money.

Jonathan.

We are not yet in a position to renew your instructor certificate and, in an attempt to manage your expectations, it is unlikely to happen in the immediate future. You should also be aware that it is significantly important that we receive an appropriate reference from _all_ those we approach – being that you provided their names and in so doing vouched that they knew you well, as silence from any one of them often indicates more than it might otherwise suggest.

In your particular case there are also EASA implications to the (colloquially known) 'fit and proper' category of person following your conviction and subsequent sentence and it is clearly important that we follow their requirements.

I will look more closely into your file during the course of next week.

Best regards

Thanks for that _____,

Do you want me to chase ___ or shall I leave it to you? I stress that I have only known ___ *since* my imprisonment – we got involved over our interest in prison reform. I am certain that I made this clear at our meeting.

Jonathan.

The Justice Minister (Part Seven)

12 April 2013

Hi

Apologies for the delay. This week has been exceptionally busy. I will give you a call early next week, as I am away from the office today.

Thanks

(Author: He didn't call.)

The CAA (Part Three)

12 April 2013

Inbound

Thank you but no, we will deal with it from our end.

Best regards

Outbound

OK. Thank you. Please keep me in the loop. I am keen to resolve this.

Best

Jonathan.

Inbound

Noted.

Best regards

The Justice Minister (Part Eight)

29 April 2013

Despite an assurance at the conclusion of our meeting in March that the MoJ would be in touch I had received the square-route of not a lot in return. A few emails promising a phone call – which never materialised and then, miracle of miracles, a text message promising me a call in the morning.

No call came.

Behind the scenes however, I was getting wind – whispers – that something was afoot in the Ministerial mandate… something speculative that would be good for prisoners who wanted to teach others to read was crystallising. A game-changing breakthrough…

The CAA (Part Four)

7 May 2013

Outbound

Dear _____,

Can you please let me know if you have had any luck with ___ _____ MP. Following my appearance on *Any Answers* over the weekend I am attending Westminster again (mid-month) to meet the Shadow MoJ and would like to chase if he still has not come back to you.

Inbound

I will find out – my belief is that we are still to hear from him. I will know more tomorrow.

Best regards

Outbound

Thank you. He is RUBBISH at responding. He still has not corrected his spelling error from his blog of mid March that I flagged for him.

As per your instruction I have NOT communicated with him re CAA stuff – only prison issues.

The Prison Ombudsman (Part Two)

9 May 2013

Dear Mr Robinson

Thank you for your letter which we received on 2 April 2013.

I apologise for not replying sooner but this is due to my enquiries with HMP Hollesley Bay taking longer than expected.

You have asked the Prison and Probation Ombudsman to consider your complaint about an incident that happened in the Education Department on 1 September 2011 when you were in Hollesley Bay.

The Ombudsman's office can only investigate complaints within a year of the original incident occurring.

We can only investigate complaints once the Prison Services' internal complaints procedure has been completed. As I am sure you can appreciate, if it is a long time after the event it can be very difficult to decide the truth of any evidence which is still available. In your case, the original incident happened on 1 September 2011 and there is no evidence that you have completed the Prison Services' internal complaints procedure. We therefore cannot investigate this matter.

Once again, I would like to apologise for not being in a position to let you know this sooner.

Author: It appears – to me – that the Ombudsman required more than a month to calculate that September 1st, 2011 was more than one calendar year ago.

Various letters went back and forth subsequent to the receipt of the above. My MP got involved too. It was voraciously pointed out that complaints *were* made – on the *afternoon of the barring of Toe by Toe* as logged within IN IT – and for that matter, during my remaining time at the Bay I would constantly nag 'Frank' – the ex-prison officer of Tribal – whom the Head of Education had referred me to following his in-house sabotage.

The Ombudsman cited the 'difficult economic climate' being the stumbling block to further investigation – despite the fact that our side was trying to flag money being poured down the drain at the Bay.

To save the Ombudsman time and motion it was eventually hinted that the most economic method of substantiating events would be a simple phone call to 'Frank' to confirm what happened.

The Ombudsman never replied to this request.

House of Commons

Thursday 9 May 2013

The House met at half-past Nine o'clock

PRAYERS

[Mr Speaker *in the Chair*]

Sir Edward Garnier (Harborough) (Con): Will he also urge the people he deals with to ensure that people are able to read when they leave prison? The average prisoner has the reading age of an 11-year-old and it is not possible for them to get a job if they cannot read.

Chris Grayling: I agree with my hon. and learned Friend. His point about reading is of great importance. I want to see those prisoners who can read teaching those who cannot to do so.

The Justice Minister (Part Nine)

9 May 2013

I watched the above speech by the Justice Minister on television. I'm afraid to report that when he told the House of Commons that able-worded prisoners must teach their illiterate colleagues their ABC's I let rip – the toys went out of the pram. As my goggle box was severely shouted at the phone was reached for. A pounding furious text was sent to my man at the Ministry asking what the hell they were up to.

Amazingly, he rang me back almost straight away. The dialogue:

CALLER

Um... Er... Hello Jonathan. I got your text...Um...

JR

(Remembering manners – but seething) *Thank you for FINALLY calling. What the HELL was that about? You know DAMN well stopped me from teaching prisoners to read.*

CALLER

Yes. We thought that might hit a nerve. Sorry.

JR

Sorry?!!! What bloody good is that? When are you lot going to face up to the fact that deliberately put the kibosh on teaching prisoners to read in an open resettlement prison for God's sake? What the hell are you playing at?

CALLER

Um… Er… I can't really talk now. I'm with Chris at the House. I'll call you.

Irate – still – I went out for a walk to cool off. Christ I was angry.

Sorry to be dramatic but JEEEZ.

The night before this *The Apprentice* had been watched on telly. During which Lord Sugar told one team that the trick was 'to deploy people in tasks they were good at'. At HMP Hollesley Bay I was, I believe, the *only* Toe by Toe mentor within the boundaries during my stay…

During the Justice Minister's declaration today to the House he also sprouted such gems as 'the system needs to be more creative with less money being spent…be more innovative' and that the 'system is terrible value for the tax payer'.

I tried my best to do something positive during my much merited sentence. The irony of the Minister's rhetoric of 'utilising the voluntary sector' mixed with the 'ability to read greatly important to prisoners' and the final comment of tax payers' money must 'actually make a difference' made me think of a certain company that during 2012/2013 trousered £7,751,340,00 from the people's repository – and that derisory sum just for the education services they provide in our jails…

MACKAY

What are you doing Fletcher?

FLETCHER

[Holding TV above head – about to throw it at JARVIS] *Just adjusting the television Mr Mackay.*

MACKAY

With the set above your head?

FLETCHER

Yes, it's the vertical hold.

The CAA (Part Five)

10 May 2013

Inbound

Dear Mr Robinson,

I write again, as you requested that you were 'kept in the loop' with any developments.

We wrote again to Mr _____ MP on 22 April 2013. This followed a letter that we also sent to him in December 2012. To date, we have not received a response to either. As indicated previously to you, whilst not wishing to pre-judge the meaning of this, a 'nil' response can often indicate a disinclination to supply a character reference, for reasons various.

Clearly we do not have the time nor inclination to chase but, without suitable references, especially where they are needed to assert and confirm your 'fitness' in terms of behaviour, character and honesty, we are unable to progress this further.

A combination of the requirements contained within EASA Part ARA and CAP 804 Part 1 [Flight Crew Licensing: Mandatory Requirements] also make provision for further restrictions/terms following events such that you have experienced. This, in effect, relates to sanctions and time periods before which you can be considered for either and instructor or examiner certificates. As such it is likely that without corroborative and 'glowing' character references from responsible and respected public officials, that know you well, it would not be likely that we would consider you in the instructor role for some time yet.

I say this to you now so that you can manage your expectations along those lines. Traditionally, those time frames have been in the order of 2 or 3 years in circumstances such as yours.

I hope you feel that this brings you up to date for the time being.

Best regards

Outbound

Dear _____,

Thanks for that.

Is it OK if I chase him then?

Jonathan

Of course but should you do so, please advise him that we will also need to speak with him and seek supportive evidence of his comments. It is not your involvement with the prison service that is of interest to us particularly – it is more fundamental than that as I am sure your are aware.

Best regards

Understood! Will get on the case.

Thanks for your help.

Jonathan.

The Writing MP (Part Five)

13 May 2013

Outbound

Hi _____,

Good to talk to you.

As explained in our telecon the CAA have been chasing ___ for a warts-and-all observation on where I am and have not managed to get hold of him.

Their comments are attached.

I know ___ is very busy but if you could get him to say something – good or bad! – it would help me big time.

I have made it VERY clear to the CAA that I have only known ___ SINCE prison but that he would confirm that A: I have not reoffended (to the best of his knowledge!) and B: that I have been doing nothing other than working on prison reform.

Hope all is well with you.

I am back at Westminster on the 20th to meet the Shadow MOJ mob.

Best,

Jonathan.

CC: The CAA.

Hi Jonathan,

Thanks for the email and good to talk to you earlier.

I have had a dig around and have found the letter of 22 April from ____ _____ at the CAA. ___ would be happy to give a reference and will try and send it today or tomorrow. He had previously not been in touch due to an unprecedented workload with the local elections on top which had taken over. He sends his apologies for the lack of a reply.
Best wishes,

CC: CAA

Hi _____,

That's great news, thank you very much – to you both.

The CAA implied that the silence was ominous – I did try and explain ___'s workload and that he probably just needed a prod!

Please pass my thanks to him – and get him to correct the spelling on his blog of early March!

I'll let you know how I get on with Shadow MoJ.

Best,

Jonathan.

CC: CAA

The Shadow Prison Minister

20 May 2013

That same hackneyed Albert Finney Coffee bar. Big Ben on my right. Portcullis House on my left. Here I was again. My MP – now a vital ally – had made arrangements for me to meet the opposition *Porridge* Minister. A lady – who pre-politics had worked for some time within clink circles. I had read up on her and gathered she knew her onions – and tins of tuna.

Security hoops successfully concluded, I waited to meet someone of influence hoping that the outcome would be more satisfactory than my last ubiquitous liaison here.

A female assistant arrived – smiley, who announced she had read my book. Her first question as she escorted me to meet HRH was – assuming that ON IT would have the same format as IN IT – if she could be Marilyn Monroe. I answered in my best Clark Gable that there were no stars in the sequel.

There was a bit of pouting on that.

The Shadow Minister had some Kate Bush about her. We sat down in the same dining area that my last two meetings had taken place in. The arena was in a quieter state of grace than on previous visits. Possibly connected to the fact that the night before there had been a fight in the bar between some saturated MP's and one of them had been dragged away by the police in handcuffs.

I am *not* making this up.

In the post punch-up tranquillity Ms Bush announced we had slightly less than an hour as she had to go and vote on something – and then checked with another aware aide (who was gorgeous) that the timing of said appointment was correct. Everyone had electronic tablets and as the nominated hour was clarified it was like being on the bridge of the *USS Enterprise* such was the beeping.

Phasers were set to business. Across the table sat (Gorgeous) aide, Ms Bush and Ms Monroe. I won't bore you with the details – you've heard them all already. It was the same Carthaginian-sacking manifesto as before; the appallingly phenomenal – bordering on farce – surreal degree of apathy witnessed in prison that had taken my breath away – and associated hokum. I concluded with events of colliding with a private education providing (?) company and being turfed-out of producing purposeful activity at HMP Holiday Bay via teaching prisoners to read, known to reduce reoffending. I went a tad further by voicing that I was more than a little surprised that *no one* was doing anything about this. Could she help me? Could she raise some parliamentary question or something?

"No, I won't – it takes too much time." GOD GIVE ME STRENGTH, internalised I.

What came next *finally* hit the nail home in this bear of little brain that if I was going to get *anything* done about the complete shambles that is our prison system, I was on my own…

"Jonathan, no one doubts for *one second* that everything in your book didn't happen. The problem is that the prison system is a *burning building* and *everyone* wants to look the other way. *Especially* politicians."

I can't remember the rest of the conversation. There was some small talk. I was too stunned by having doggedly got to the ramshackle top – meetings with MoJ management and now the Shadow section – and got nowhere at all. The law of diminishing returns I suppose. Ms Bush went off to vote and I sat, agog, with Monroe and Gorgeous.

They both studied me.

Pause.

I told them tooth and claw I wasn't going to stop. This isn't on. I deserved jail but what I saw going on isn't good enough. It's imprisonment by numbers. Why does Westminster have in its roots such sundry contempt at clink concerns whilst Nero fiddles? Why does the subject so seldom attract rethinking? All I get is ambling rhetoric. All the public get is crass covering-up-the-cracks spiel too – and new buttons never did make a new suit.

There's loads of Dunkirk spirit potential embedded among the ne'er-do-well prison populace – in skillset *spades* – but it's essentially not being encouraged. Worse, often it's not only not ebbed-on but sometimes even discombobulated discouraged. This frittering is nonsensical madness. The Elton John song with *that* line:

The honey the hive could be holding.

Gorgeous and Monroe looked at me like I was a loon. I thanked them for their time and left.

Befuddled – and not overly thrilled with my less-than-stellar progress I went and stood under the lee of Big Ben bewildered. Some soul searching thinking took place. Quite a lot of hard mulling. This felon's thoughts pitched and fell on the oceans of notion. Yes, you cocked up your life – causing supreme mayhem for others and yes prison was reflectively inevitable. Cards on table: tried to take it on the chin and 'do the right thing' but the bloody toxic system didn't let me. How many other times has this happened? Why won't the management man-up and acknowledge it is wrong? Why is it so hyper sensitively profoundly prickly? No wonder prison doesn't work. One would have thought jug jurisdiction would have advanced from growing pains by now.

The enmeshing looking-the-other-way by the alliance of Westminster encompassing resolute priggishness, whilst more than I bargained for, indubitably had a profound effect on me.

Prison proprietors' perpetual preposterous propensity prowess – almost to a man – of not floating – or making anywhere near any effort to re-float the still buoyant wreckage, salvaging the possible turnaround of offenders – some *laced* with potential – so lavishly displayed through scintillating camaraderie – in jail, is just *Monty Python*. The existing merging of punishment and rehabilitation is an oil and water mismatch. Rehabilitation in prison, is merely along for the ride.

And political posturing politicians – ministerial monuments – when not routinely spurting pandering pretence prison-press platitude phenomenal piecemeal pragmatism PR parlance would sooner chew razor blades than admit that.

Until prison, per se, rebukes the fixation of naysayers and embarks on a new heading by upping its game on *in-house* rehabilitation – utilising the chief assets on offer packed to the gunwales already in its fiefdom – currently redundant – by firing up the stove, it will ultimately remain the lurid imbued adept epic fail that it is, no less. The existing dire situation devoid of success needs to get its reoffending house in order. Currently, it doesn't even have housemaid's knee. Rehabilitation in prison? Blink-and-you'd-miss-it.

Reality hammered home: Right Robinson. You really are on your own.

Elton again:

From here on sonny, sonny, sonny, it's a long and lonely climb.

The Judge

21 May 2013

Having blurted to all glitterati involved in the prison reform crowd that I was *more* than interested in attending *anything* concerned with the movement – a *hunger* to do right – I found myself sitting in a students' lecture amphitheatre one blisteringly warm evening. A debate was held. The panel front of house consisted of various figureheads of high rank all connected in matters CJS.

One was a retired Judge. And had something – of importance – to do with some prison education committee or other. My gaze was firmly centred on him… At some juncture during the dialogue he was asked about prison education. He told the gathering that he had taken many fellow Judges into prisons to see "education in progress…"

He was slowly shaking his head as he uttered those *mot juste* words.

At the aftermath of the discussion we were all invited to wine and nibbles in an adjacent chamber. The Judge was pounced on. My history was rattled-off and the subject matter of a recently released book was revealed. It was communicated that I was desperate to talk to him about what I had – not – witnessed in the surreal prison education stakes during my imprisonment. Would he talk with me?

"Young man, (I liked the 'young' bit) I will gladly talk to you. But only if you get me a drink first." The bar was manoeuvred to with pace that would shame Fleet Street of old at opening time. His sauce of preference was a glass of red. As the barman poured the Claret my eyeballs were glued to my source of prison education hierarchy. Bordeaux in hand, I boarded-down on His Honour.

He seemed most relieved to be given a drink. Fifty shades of *Rumpole* whiplashed through my mind. As he breathed the bouquet, the poor man got more broadsides from me. He interrupted – I suppose Judges can do that – and asked what I had done to be sent to jail. All was told. "Well, the first thing I will say is that if you had been in my court there's no way I would have sent you to prison." At this point it was *very* firmly communicated that I didn't want anyone to think that was my issue. My beef concerns the intrinsic appalling wasted opportunity of rehabilitation *in* prison, the mesmeric shooting-down of peer to peer mentoring – I threw in mentors are quadruple their net worth – because goals are clearly vested within and the lamentable lack of leadership from a completely disinterested staff. All of this, I explained, I have tried to communicate from my past vantage point in a certain book – it attempts to scream this out. Please could I send him a copy? I went on – in full flow: For instance, In Norway, prison officers are trained for two years, here it's a matter of weeks. Compare the reoffending rates…

The Judge deliberating his verdict sipped his wine.

"Young man, I will gladly read your book – send it to me. However your figures are incorrect. Officers are not trained for two years in Norway."

Another taste of wine was consumed before he passed further sentence.

"It's three years."

The CAA (Part Six)

30 May 2013

Outbound

Hello ____,

Can you please let me know if you have heard from ___ yet?

Regards,

Jonathan.

Inbound

No

Best regards

Outbound

Will chase again.

The Writing MP (Part Six)

30 May 2013

Outbound

Hi _____,

Just checked with the CAA if they have received _____ 's letter and got a no.

Can you please drop me an email with an update.

Best,

Jonathan.

CC: CAA

Inbound

Jonathan,

He hasn't sent it yet I am afraid – very hectic here. He is up North currently but back here on Monday so I will make sure he sends it then.

Sorry for the delay!

Outbound

No prob. Can you drop me an email when he has please!

Met with Shadow MoJ last week – ask ___ to give me a buzz when he has a mo.

Best

JR

Inbound

Will do.

Michael Spurr, Chief Executive NOMS.

1 June 2013

Dear Mr Spurr,

I hope this reaches you – I am sure you get bombarded with copious quantities of correspondence on matters prison but this is important. I'll try and keep this brief:

Idiot helicopter instructor steals money from employer and gets imprisoned (quite rightly) in July of 2011 for 15 months. Ends up serving 17 weeks or so and is released on HDC.

During my incardination 320,000 words were penned in a fly-on-the-wall manner and released as IN IT on March 5th of this year.

I was horrified by what I saw going on – or rather, not going on – in prison and am doing my best to raise awareness of the shambles in clink. Plot lines vary from prison officers asleep on duty, vast quantities of drugs everywhere all the way through to the unfathomable barring of Toe by Toe (peer-to-peer teaching of reading) by a Mr _____ _____ (of ___) at HMP Hollesley Bay. The latter particularly guiling after Chris Grayling's recent address to the House of Commons that "prisoners who can read must teach those who can't."

I am writing to you because I would very much like you to read my book. I wonder if you could kindly respond with an email address I can send a PDF version to, or a postal address to dispatch a disc to.

Mr Grayling's office has a copy of IN IT. This explains the greenish colour occupants of his department have gone.

(Author: NOMS acknowledged receipt of this communication but no reply ever materialised).

The Prison Reform Trust (Part Four)

4 June 2013

Jeremy Wright: But it seems to be clear that the crime we have got is committed repeatedly by the same people. So reoffending has to be the focus of what we do. It is because of the reoffending rates, which we all agree are too high, that we have tried to look again at the provision of rehabilitation, and what we would like to do differently. I don't need to tell anybody here what those rates are: 50% for those leaving custody overall, 60% for those leaving custody after short sentences – that is the percentage for those who have reoffended within a year of leaving prison – and 70% of young offenders leaving custody. Those figures are of course far too high, so there is a clear need to make some changes, and to drive those rates down. That is what we seek to do.

It is important to avoid the perverse incentives around rehabilitation work that is done unimaginatively. We wanted see good new ideas coming into this space. We are very conscious that a lot of those good new ideas will come from the voluntary sector.

I am very conscious that as the minister responsible for prisons, and indeed for rehabilitation and probation, there is always a danger that when you talk about one you forget about the other. This has to be a process of rehabilitation that is continuous, from inside the prison, through the prison gate and out into the community. That means that you must not forget about what happens inside prison. Going backwards in the process, then, you will have picked up that there have been some changes to the Incentives and Earned Privileges (IEP) scheme that operates within prisons. The fundamental purpose for doing that is to make sure that every incentive, every lever we have within prison, is directed towards rehabilitation. Up to this point, we have had an IEP system which is largely about staying out of trouble and being rewarded for that. Now of course it is important that prisoners don't punch the officers, or smash up their cells, and I want to make sure that those incentives remain within the system. But, just as important, if we are arranging, as we are, a whole range of rehabilitation services to support people in changing their lives, the least we can expect is that they do their bit. So whilst in prison we want to be clear with prisoners that if you want to earn your privileges, you must of course keep your nose clean and not punch the officers, but you must also engage in rehabilitation. You must also engage in education, in work, in drug treatment, in whatever it is you need to do in order to turn your life around. If you do those things and you engage in that rehabilitation then you will be able to access those additional privileges. If you don't, you won't.

Past Prison Passion

4 June 2013

Hello,

I had not forgotten to drop you a line – I was waiting until I had finished IN IT (200 pages to go). I am finding it rather gripping, but am limited to reading it in the evenings. Keeps making me smile as I can identify with lots of it, especially the lazy disinterested officers!

I joined the prison service in 1971 and was sent to _____ Borstal as a green 21 year old, I kept hearing the term 'Cherry' when Borstal boys were about, after a couple of months I asked one what that word meant and got the reply "It's you sir, you go red every time someone speaks to you!" In those days everyone was employed, staff supervised work parties and were attached to a specific wing so continuity was important and you were in contact with the same prisoners throughout their sentence. In 1987 management decided overtime should stop and a new working practice was introduced known as 'Fresh Start'. As a result work parties decreased, continuity did not exist as you were not aware where you would work until you started your shift. With lack of continuity disinterest takes over as you would not see a prisoner on successive shifts.

In 1978 I became a Catering officer and remained in that roll until I retired in 2010, I finished as a Senior officer at _____ thereby spending all 40 years with Young Offenders. I became quite famous as a no no-nonsense person and was told on a number of occasions that I was just like Alan Sugar. Often on meetings away I would be approached by staff saying "I have been waiting to meet you for years". I prided myself in my prisoners and would hand pick them. I could walk in a room of 20 prospective workers maybe requiring 4, look each one in the face and pick them without exchanging a word and would rarely make a mistake. Never employed a smoker if I could help it as they are addicts and open to bribery and the ones I did I would wean them off it. Taught many to read and Foreign Nationals to speak English. About 5 years ago I was asked to take a severely deaf prisoner with no speech; I shunted him to the mess. One weekend one of my boys said the deaf lad wanted to work the weekend and I said OK. This was his turning point as he worked hard, me and the kitchen party learned sign language, it was said he was dyslexic and a lost cause, I had a brain wave and introduced him to the computer to have a conversation, he then learned how to spell and was not dyslexic or backward at all just locked in a silent world and written off. When he reached 21, I got him to _____ and instead of sending him in a sweatbox, was allowed to take him in a taxi to hand him over personally to the lifer unit.

I also took Foreign Nationals under my wing and taught them English and how to read it, mostly Albanians, I still keep in touch with some and a Libyan and Estonian keep in touch on the web. I have a folder full of letters and cards from prisoners and their parents showing their appreciation. One has kept in touch from 1971 and says I never forgot you, he now has a successful building firm and a string of properties in _____.

Unfortunately I had more interest in the prisoners than a lot of the staff who had no interest, hated the job and were more interested in reading the paper (What the fuck are you doing in this job). There is lots more I could tell you but time defeats me and have a lawn to mow.

I will write again when I have finished your book.

Future Prison Passion

I'm reading IN IT. Mostly on the bus when I'm going to work. I'm at the bit where you are on Wilford. You've been there a while – you're trying to sort out a house for your tag. The book is making me laugh – and *think*. I don't understand why the Head of Education had a problem with you teaching Toe by Toe. Learning to read is really useful – so is helping other prisoners. They don't have many skills. I can't and don't understand why he stopped you. It's criminal.

I've recently finished University. I did my degree in Law and Criminology. This after getting four A levels including law and psychology. I have a huge interest in the CJS. Law, offending and stopping reoffending. I always wanted to be a lawyer – from about the age of ten in fact – I like *CSI* and stuff like that! I'm interested in crime. When I was choosing my degree I found criminology a lot more interesting than law. Plus, the people doing law were really snobby. They look down on you!

After I graduated I applied – looking for anything – to get into the field. I applied to probation but fell at the last hurdle because I didn't have any experience with offenders. I looked at the NOMS website and tried for a job – the one below prison officers. I can't remember what the role is called now. I did some tests and got through but was then told (*ages* later) that the job wasn't there anymore. So, at the same time as that I applied to be a prison officer – going for a job that was advertised; a vacancy at ____ prison, which is an hour on the train away from me. I applied on-line. The stuff they wanted me to fill in was very basic – much less complicated than the previous role I had applied for but didn't get. That had asked me about integrity and the like. There was none of that this time round. Anyway, I applied there and then, if that makes sense. It took about ten/fifteen minutes. I gave them all my details. I got an acknowledgement, then a week or two later – I can't remember exactly – I received an email saying that I had passed the first stage and that I needed to do – by a certain date – two tests.

I completed these on-line a few days later. A maths test and an English test. I estimate the standard – the yardstick – of the tests to equate to that of an average 15 year old. It wasn't hard work. I did both exams in one hit. I think I had fifty minutes to complete each one. I used the full time – but only because I double checked everything. I think each test had about fifteen questions. The process didn't say whether my answers were correct or not. At the end it didn't tell me my score – just a 'thank you and we will be in touch'.

House of Commons

Jeremy Wright: Absolutely right. There is already some very good peer-to-peer mentoring that is going on, a lot of good work on reading, for example, with prisoners teaching other prisoners to read through Toe by Toe and other very worthwhile schemes. The more of that that we want to see.

BUNNY

I've got this letter, like.

FLETCHER

From a woman, it looks like, and judging by the handwriting and stationery, a woman of low standards.

BUNNY

That's right. It's from the wife.

FLETCHER

Advice to the lovelorn, you want, is it? Compose an appropriate reply?

BUNNY

No, it's simpler than that Fletch. I just want you to read it to me.

Past Prison Passion (Part Two)

June 2013

Thought I would drop you a line and bore you with another chapter before I have an hour with your book, innit.

Just outside _____ was an open YOI called _____, this came under _____until the early 80's when _____was rebuilt and it was handed to ____. The Catering officer was a single post and as there were 2 of us at _____ we had to cover his absences. Although the estate was small, the civilian gardener there was brilliant, he would grow anything and they had an old fashioned greenhouse heated with pipes from the boiler room. _____ would get me to draw up a list and in the season I would pick stuff fresh and cook it. Often there would be the inmates queuing on one side of the hot plate and the staff queuing on the other. Every Saturday I would make a chicken curry with homemade onion

Bhajis and Peshwari naans. It used to go down a storm and the P.O. would come in for a plateful and say it's not a good curry unless the sweat runs off one's nose... and it did.

I used to run a cookery class one night a week, uncertificated but I always had a waiting list. Choux pastry, chocolate éclairs, jam donuts, Victoria sponge, bread rolls all over a six week cycle. Occasionally I would ring my mate the PEI and say fancy canoeing this afternoon and I would take my kitchen boys down to the scout place in _____ and have the time of our lives then come back and cook tea. I have plenty of photo's somewhere. In the Autumn I would get there early and go mushroom picking, field mushrooms, puffballs and Ink Caps and do my boys and the non-smoking staff a fried breakfast, those were the days!

In 1992 they asked me to work there permanently so I did and then they closed the bloody place down in 1994 and I went to _____ on detached duty. The cook there was shite, old fashioned methods and it was basically slops. I just did it my way and was lambasted and accused of being "The prisoners' friend". After 8 weeks I was approached by the Governor who said "Mr _____ everyone is raving about your food will you stay permanently?" So I did and after about 12 months the S.O. was kicked out and I was promoted and took over. It was a flagship, I was even headhunted by the area manager but said no.

In your book you mention the feeding allowance.

From 2006 I was on £2.25 per head then the civilian idiot running _____ wanted to make a name for himself and said he could do it for £1.91. They believed him and put everyone on that and nearly every prison was overspent, then they gave the contract to who had no idea what the requirements were required to feed a prison and last year _____ were £50k overspent in the kitchen.

Future Prison Passion (Part Two)

A few weeks later – it was about a month actually – I received an email saying that I had passed and could I please attend an assessment centre. I was given the option to choose which one I wanted to go to. I went two or three weeks later. It was in London. There wasn't one near me. I got the overnight coach because the train would have cost about £___. I rang them to see if they would put any money towards it but they wouldn't (they wouldn't even provide food on the day apart from tea and coffee) so it was the bus for me! I couldn't afford a hotel so overnight travel was the only option.

I took food with me. I didn't sleep much on the bus – there was a screaming baby giving it some so sleep was impossible. I got into London at about five o'clock in the morning and arrived at the assessment centre at about half past seven after two tubes and a bus across London. I was really early – I was there before the staff got there! When they turned up they said "why are you here? You're really early. You can't come in yet". Fine, I told them. It was only because I didn't know where I was going and I wanted to make sure I got there on time. They wouldn't let me in the building – not even for a cup of tea. It was my fault for being too early.

Eventually they let me in. I was given a badge. I went upstairs and was told what was going to happen and then was instructed to go and sit and wait for everyone else to arrive. Whilst I was waiting I had to get a medical examination done. I was given some forms to fill out. I had filled out loads of forms before this which I had taken down with me. They went through stuff to make sure I had filled it out properly. It was all about 'are you married' and 'who to'. They wanted family details and everything. Not an issue. Fair enough. They wanted my mum's history – my dad's history, checking on terrorism and stuff like that.

By the time everyone had turned up – we were about 20-30 in total, with a wide age-group but most were men in their mid 20's – we were then told that different things would be happening in different groups. Most of the men there already worked in prisons – in that role that's one down from an officer – the one I had applied for in the past.

The first thing I had to do, after the medical, was some tests. Basically it was the same tests I had done on-line. I think it was exactly the same questions as before, the same papers, to make sure you hadn't cheated, that you had filled out the originals yourself. I did the exams but didn't get told the results. After that they told me to go back to the waiting room.

The next thing was like a problem solving test. It's hard to explain. There were four different rooms and in each one there was a different scenario. In the first one there was a prisoner. He wasn't happy about something. I can't remember what it was. He was quite in-your-face, shouting at you. The test was how you dealt with it.

The next one was with a more senior colleague, who was trying to get you to do all the paperwork and stuff that he should have been doing. He was a bit 'dodgy' and they wanted to see how I reacted to that.

The third one was a woman – a visitor – who had travelled a hundred miles – but was not on time for published visiting hours and 'why couldn't she come in now?' So it was 'how do you deal with that?'

The last one was deciding which jobs to give which prisoners. The person doing the test was saying "let's give the worst jobs to the sex-offenders – and people like that – and give the good jobs to the others." I had to say that's not fair. You shouldn't judge people for what they've done. Everything was recorded so they could see how I reacted.

I was not tested on my newspaper reading capabilities.

After the scenario situations there was a fitness test. There was one when you had to sprint up and down the room, against a bleeping time-keeper. Then I had to squeeze something a number of times, exerting the same pressure. Next there was a pulley thing you had to pull. You had to do that five times, making sure it went over a certain number. Then a pushy one – the same sort of thing. The final task was a test with a riot shield.

You had to hold the shield at a certain angle over your head for a minute.

Past Prison Passion (Part Three)

6 June 2013

Still reading IN IT.

Prisoners used to say 'innit' in the wrong context and I had many conversations trying to correct them (in vain I may add), it eventually became the norm and spread across the estate.

You are right I have slipped through, many Governor grades used to come to me to pick my brains, since retiring I could give lots of advice but never asked, I was only a minion in uniform!

Future Prison Passion (Part Three)

We had all been told that we'd be there until five o'clock but I actually finished at one o'clock. You're not supposed to talk to the other applicants about what's happening in each room but afterwards I was chatting to a guy in my group about how he had dealt with it. He already worked for the service and said he'd done this, that and whatever, professional jargon which I had never heard of – because no one had told me. I said I didn't know any of that stuff because I don't work in a prison. I didn't know that those things were available.

I was a bit annoyed about that. I wanted to have a *fair* opportunity. This guy knew a lot more about the prison workings than I did. For instance, the lady who had travelled miles for a visit – this guy was able to offer her a solution – but I didn't know that there was a solution available.

I had dressed up to the nines – smart dress, high heels, for a proper job interview. I thought at some point I'm going to get a proper one-on-one interview. It didn't happen. When they told me I was done I was really surprised that no one had talked to me directly. I asked what happens next. They said that they would be in touch to let me know if I had been successful or not. What then? I asked. "Well, if there's a place for you, we'll ask you if you still want the job or not. If yes, you'll go onto the job, if not you've got a year from the day you applied for a job, to see if anything comes up in that time."

I hung about for a bit because the coach I could have got, but didn't go for – because I had to pre-book my travel – was at five o'clock and I never thought I'd make that, so I'd booked the next one which was ten o'clock. So I went for something to eat with the guy from my group.

I later heard from him that although he already worked for the prison service, he wasn't successful. Anyway, he told me that people who already worked for the service, got all their travel and stuff paid for.

I got home at one o'clock in the morning.

The Writing MP (Part Seven)

A week passed with nothing being heard from Westminster with regard to the promised reference for me. My ticket back to flying. They had assured me they would drop an email my way when the deed had been done – in between my one-man-band prison reform stuff, I was more than keen to at least keep the aviation door open, the primary method of earning an income. I felt odd about a possible return – I still do – I want prisons to make sense (for all parties) before I head skywards – but I was aware helicopters were a safety net for me income-wise. This after all, had been repeated to me over and over by the prison contingent whilst I was in jail. Employment is a key issue in reducing reoffending.

The CAA had insisted references landed their way before allowing me to launch. Fair enough. The Writing MP had said he'd give me one. His office had assured me they would alert me when it had been done. I hadn't heard anything. I rang _____ , the MP's assistant.

He was cagey. The conversation went *exactly* as follows:

JR

Sorry to hound you – but the silence isn't helping me at all with the CAA – and you did say that you would kindly let me know when _____ had sent his promised email to the CAA.

ASSISTANT

Er...

JR

Is there a problem?

ASSISTANT

Well actually yes. The Party Chairman has advised _____ not to give you a reference. Sorry.

JR

But _____ promised. You've seen the emails from the CAA indicating that his silence is ominous. They have said my future in flying depends on what he says. He said he would. You said he would.

ASSISTANT

Well your MP wrote you a reference.

JR

Yes I know, but the CAA said they wanted two references – you've seen the emails.
You've emailed me promising me that would. The CAA probably think I sent myself those emails. _____
was always quick to ask me for my help. I even got Jonathan Aitken to come along to _____ 's function.
The CAA have told me his reluctance means something.
This isn't fair.

ASSISTANT

Sorry, can't help.

Once off the line I contacted the MP direct asking him to call me. I have not heard from the Right Honourable Member or his assistant since.

The CAA (Part Seven)

6 June 2013

Hello _____,

I have just chased _____ MP again for the reference you have requested before the CAA considers it acceptable whether or whether not I (one day) return to aviation.

_____, his assistant has told me that the Party Chairman has instructed ___ not to issue a reference – despite various emails saying that such a communication would be forthcoming.

I can only assume that this is because of the war I am waging against the government approved agency whose actions during my (well deserved) punishment I am now making a severe fuss about.

_____ said to me that 'they have a reference from _____'. I acknowledged this but flagged your past comment that ____'s silence could be read as ominous.

I am thus – I think – stuck.

Can you please advise me what you want me to do.

Best,

Jonathan.

Past Prison Passion (Part Four)

10 June 2013

Hi,

Hollesley Bay had the largest farm on the prison estate, it supplied fresh vegetables and processed veg to all prisons in the south of England. It also supplied bedding plants and cut flowers to those prisons. It had (maybe still has) the best Suffolk Punch equine stud in England. Its veg processing plant employed many prisoners, its demise came about through the numerous complaints re the standard of processed potatoes.

They were shocking believe me, half were thrown away son in about 1998 the supply of vegetables was put out to contract.

When I started at _____ there was a 500 pig farm producing top quality pork and bacon, also a field producing cabbage and Poly tunnels full of salad crops. All sadly gone and put out to contract costing millions of pounds to the taxpayer that used to be carried out by prison labour.

Staff did not have the luxury of sitting around drinking tea and reading papers because they were busy supervising working parties.

As I said before all this came to an end when 'Fresh Start' was introduced. Lack of continuity brings about boredom and lack of interest in your daily charges. The introduction of female staff in male prisons was another bad idea, at _____ there has been one female staff-member imprisoned for falling pregnant by a prisoner and at least a dozen dismissed for improper relationships with prisoners.

When I joined it was advertised as a career for life with a good pension, a free house with all maintenance including decoration carried out by works staff. Now on the application form the applicant is asked how long they are anticipating staying in the job 1, 3 or 5 years hence the wrong people are being employed plus the fact the salary has been reduced from 25k down to 17k and the abolition of London weighting payments.

Beam me up Scottie!

Future Prison Passion (Part Four)

A month later I got an email from them saying that I had been successful. It also told me my marks and what the pass-rates had been for each item. The grades were A to E; C was the pass-rate. I got C's and one A.

That was the last I heard from the prison service.

Since then, I changed my mind about becoming a prison officer. That is until I read IN IT, which has made me think that I *would* like to do it and go in and be a *good* prison officer. It makes me angry that from what I've read in your book that they are not doing their job properly.

I believe the primary purpose of prison officers is to make sure there is order to the day. Prisons are to protect the public – and to punish offenders. They are also supposed to rehabilitate them...

BRIDGER

Last night, Mr Governor, my toilet was broken into.

GOVERNOR

Toilet?

BRIDGER

Toilet.

GOVERNOR

Broken into?

BRIDGER

Broken into.

GOVERNOR

Well, I'm... terribly sorry.

BRIDGER

There are some places which, to an Englishman, are sacred.

GOVERNOR

Well, I've apologised, Bridger.

BRIDGER

And so you should have. You are not doing your job properly.
Her Majesty's prison is there not only to keep people getting out, but to prevent people getting in.
You are symptomatic of the lazy, unimaginative management which is driving this country on the rocks.

Rod Redemption (Part Three)

When he called the thing that hit me most was relief. *Rod was out* – again – and sounded nothing other than broken. He'd been released about ten days before he rang and explained the delay in contact simply because he hadn't had the wherewithal to top-up his phone. I did my best to express support for him and enquired what the score was. The postage-stamp explanation was that he was sofa-surfing and doing his best to secure employment. I reciprocated that these issues were vital and then as sensitively as possible made it clear-as-crystal that he needed to keep his nose as clean as a new sixpence. He graciously acknowledged this and said he would be in touch.

RED

[narrating] *There's a harsh truth to face. No way I'm gonna make it on the outside. All I do anymore is think of ways to break my parole, so maybe they'll send me back. Terrible thing, to live in fear. All I want is to be back where things make sense. Where I won't have to be afraid all the time. Only one thing stops me. A promise I made to Andy.*

The Prison Reform Trust (Part Five)

Response to NOMS Commissioning Intentions

June 2013

"For key delivery partners we would encourage greater use of strategic partnership funding arrangements, such as Toe by Toe."

The God Squad

June 2013

Hello Jonathan

As you can understand I have had to seek permission to reply to your email, because of my role within the prison, and your relatively recent time inside. So apologies for the delay.

Your time at Bedford was during my first 3 weeks as the _____ chaplain. I recognised one of my chaplaincy colleagues from your description!

Obviously your time as a prisoner gives you a unique voice, so of course I am not going to contradict your views of what was a very personal, and necessarily subjective, experience. I think I would say that I found your comments rather harsh regarding the time taken for things to happen – having worked in prisons for several years I know things do seem frustratingly slow, but I also know that I have many dedicated and caring colleagues who are managing a large workload as best as they can. As a busy local jail, serving several courts, Bedford sees over 6000 men per year through its gates. But we are always grateful for the opportunity to reflect on how we do things.

I can't comment on your time at the Bay – I have colleagues and friends there but have never worked there.

I'm glad that you found a supportive group of fellow prisoners there though, and clearly there was a lot of mutual aid going on.

I hope you are pleased with the wider reactions to your book – and I also hope that life is now in a happy new chapter for you.

Every good wish

IN IT Flashback (Part Four)

I thought I'd go and enquire if the staff could shed any light on this official documentation, to see if someone knew something that I didn't.

The Walrus was on duty in the mini-cab office but I couldn't speak to him.

Because *again* he was *fast asleep*.

Past Prison Passion (Part Five)

11 June 2013

I always used to stick up for my prisoners if I thought they were right. I have lost count of the times I chased OMU. The usual reply was "Do you know what he is in for?" I would reply "It's none of your business now get it done". They used to call me Mr Grumpy!

I had an Asian lad who was gym orderly but spent every morning 7-9 in the kitchen, 12-2 in the mess and weekends in the kitchen. He was over 21 and due for a move into the adult estate. I was off-duty and was told by a fellow staff-member "_____ is going to such and such prison because he doesn't know where to go." I told him to wait until I was back. The morning I returned he came into the kitchen and asked me "Do you know anyone at ____ prison? I might go there." I said "yes I know the Governor. She was an officer with me, you would suit the ___ unit" (a separate super enhanced wing where they all worked out). I made a call and the following day he was there. Not only that but the S.O. PEI who used to be at _____ and owed me a favour – so employed him in the gym. _____ eventually worked out at ___ Health Spa. He did so well that he now works as a Personal Trainer at their _____ branch and has more qualifications than you can shake a stick at. He once said to me "know what Mr___, I would have none of them if I was not in prison." He was a perfect prisoner, a lifer too. I always had time for lifers as they only do the crime once unlike robbers etc. who do it regularly.

Heard you on the radio. Your accent made me smile, I can imagine what the officers would say in Bedford when you turned up on the landing. It's no wonder Steptoe treated you with disdain!!!

I still keep in touch with quite a few of my ex lads now I am retired, mostly through social media and they know if they need me I am here (mentoring is not new). A few parents keep in touch too, one regularly, her son is also a lifer. He went to __ after __ on my recommendation and is now nearing the end in ___. I will tell her to get him your book.

I used to have the Governors in my pocket as they knew if a lad could be turned around I could do it. I was often asked "how do you do it, they worship the ground you walk on" the answer was simple: "I talk to them like people."

Rod Redemption (Part Four)

He sounded much better this time around. As per typical Statham productivity he'd found a job – again on a building site – and was working all the hours God gave him. Accommodation remained an issue, still camping in friends' living rooms and he asked if I could help him out with a fairly hefty deposit on a new home – which was dearer than mine. On went the advice hat; the wisdom of securing a property that sounded like it had a swimming pool, a double garage and space enough to land a helicopter was questioned. Jonathan Aitken's post-prison baby-steps strategy was – again – repeated and Rod was gently advised to look for a bedsit. Murmuring that I was 'right as usual', he promised he'd be in touch.

The God Squad (Part Two)

11 June 2013

Thanks for coming back to me – super to hear from you. How sad that the 'God squad' needs HMP permission to respond – but totally respect your position.

Glad that you clocked in IN IT whom from your mob featured.

Yes some stuff in the piece may be harsh – but it was as I found it... The spelling mistakes in the Induction paperwork – Rehabilitation?? This in the prison that during my (much deserved) stay had the highest suicide rate of any prison in England and Wales... The officer I found asleep on duty (twice) is not fit for purpose....

Post prison I have learnt that officers in Norway are trained for 3 years. Here it's six weeks...

I hope it is very clear from both the book and my campaign that I am doing my best to get change.

What I saw simply isn't good enough.

I am so grateful that you came back to me. Please, next time you are at Bedford, visit B 2 5 (You will find my dots behind the door) and tell the occupants that the tunnel of prison does have an end. And please tell B 2 5 that I made it OK.

My very best to you – and to all Chaplains in the HMP system.

Jonathan.

Past Prison Passion (Part Six)

16 June 2013

Have just finished IN IT.

It was good to see you wrote letters to the staff.

_____ (prison officer) is now reading your book and is enjoying it. He is up to the point you are about to be transferred to Hollesley Bay.

He is picking famous nicknames for the other staff like you did!

The CAA (Part Eight)

24 June 2013

Hello _____,

Sent you an email a week or so ago asking for the way forward – please can you update me!

Jonathan.

Rod Redemption (Part Five)

A far more realistically priced and sized dwelling – a bedsit – was described down the phone. That's more like it, I responded. As well as more prodding and poking on the subject of behaving himself, a bit of assistance was also thrown his way so he could move into his own place – and that's all you need to know.

RED

[narrating] *I must admit that I didn't think much of Andy first time I laid eyes on him; looked like a stiff breeze would blow him over. That was my first impression of the man.*

Chris Grayling Visits HMP Bedford

Bedfordshire on Sunday 27 June 2013

When asked about his response to former inmate of HMP Bedford Jonathan Robinson's book on life behind bars in Bedford, the Secretary said: "I regularly get emails and letters every week from former offenders with interesting ideas about how to improve the prison system, I read them with interest and ask the National Offender Management Service (NOMS) to take on what is said. It is quite unusual however to write a book about it."

The Bedford MP (Part Four)

Not surprisingly Bedford's MP accompanied the Minister on his tour around the local prison in June. I emailed him – on a number of occasions – subsequent to that walkabout.

He has not responded.

House of Commons

Tuesday 2 July 2013

The House met at half-past Eleven o'clock

PRAYERS

[Mr Speaker *in the Chair*]

Mr Raab: According to a recent Ministry of Justice survey, one in five prisoners needs help reading and writing. Charities like the Shannon Trust have pioneered peer mentoring and synthetic phonics to improve literacy rates. What steps is the Minister taking to expand such innovative programmes, and does he agree that they are absolutely crucial to equipping offenders with the skills they need to go straight on release?

Jeremy Wright: I agree with my hon. Friend. He is right to cite the Shannon Trust. Its Toe by Toe project is an extremely good example of what we are discussing. We will help it in any way we can. I hope that he will hear a little more about that over the rest of the summer. The important changes we have made to the incentives and earned privileges scheme go beyond simply what we may take away from prisoners; they are also about the incentives we give them to help other prisoners. In order to reach the enhanced level of the scheme, a prisoner will have to help someone else in prison. That is a good opportunity for more mentoring and more learning coaching of the type he describes.

Seema Malhotra (Feltham and Heston) (Lab/Co-op): How supportive is the Minister of creative agencies getting into prisons to help improve language and literacy, and is he aware of any barriers they might have experienced to running workshops in prisons?

Jeremy Wright: I am certainly in favour of anything that can be demonstrated to assist in reducing reoffending, but there is another test that needs to be applied: a public acceptability test. The public have certain expectations of what should and should not happen in prison, so we need to apply that filter, but I am certainly interested in imaginative ideas that will help to drive down reoffending rates.

Iago (Part Four)

Dear Jonathan

I do appreciate what you are attempting to do. The grit in the works is the same grit that makes the oyster, so keep going.

Time to drop the "idiot" label, that is now all history and in reality it is the last thing that you are. What you are doing now is laudable and people are listening.

Languishing in Cells

Inside Time

July 2013

Justice Minister (and former TV executive – oh the irony!): "It is not right that some prisoners appear to be spending hours languishing in their cells." Mr Grayling fails to mention the majority of prisoners are crying out for work.

The CAA (Part Nine)

3 July 2013

Inbound

Mr Robinson

I do not see the significance of this e-mail communication and ask that you desist further from copying me and my team in with information that is irrelevant to CAA business.

Best regards

Dear _____,

I did it as I have had no reply from you to my last three of four emails requesting the way forward between the CAA and me.

I was attempting to show you the work I am putting into prison reform – and you asked me to CC_____ in all emails!

Please can you let me know what the situation is.

Best,

Jonathan.

(Author: This email was never replied to).

You are not going to the Ball (Part Two)

Having for a long period over the summer heard whispers and rumours that something of consequence regarding getting illiterate prisoners reading, word reached me that the MoJ had relented having finally seen sense. I was *overjoyed*.

The details acquired of where and when the Prison Minister was going to announce that Toe by Toe was to become mandatory in all our prisons my MP's office was contacted – again – to begin exploratory excavations into getting myself onto the guest-list.

It's beyond me that during my nagging pursuit that they haven't changed their number and moved to Brazil. During the zillionth conversation I made it abundantly clear that I would behave myself – the announcement was being made in a *prison*. Any schoolboy apple orchard raiding would be both fruitless and pointless – and more vitally, damaging to the cause. I wanted to be there to witness this terrific news. They told me to leave it with them.

A phone call was received shortly afterwards – then an email – from my hub HQ, instructing me to email a gentleman at the MoJ who had told my Member of Parliament's office that they would put me on the list.

Apparently they were *most* interested in how I *knew* of the forthcoming event.

My mob just told them that I was *well-connected…*

BARTLETT

Where in God's name did you get these?

GRIFFITH

Hendley

BARTLETT

Well, where did he get them?

GRIFFITH
Well, I asked him that.

BARTLETT

What did he say?

GRIFFITH

"Don't ask."

A polite, courteous email was dispatched to the Ministry – as instructed – with my details and a request of receipt of my communication and joining instructions for the forthcoming event was asked for.

I should have guessed what was to happen next…

It was some days later when the phone rang. My MP's brigade the number that flashed. The caller's opening line: "you are not going to the ball". A letter from the Prison Minister had arrived and was read – with chuckles – down the phone before a copy was electronically sent over.

What got up my nose was not the no-way-in-*hell*-is-Robinson-coming-anywhere-*near*-this-event, but the real sting suggestion that I might volunteer my services to the Shannon Trust. I hit the *roof* – for I had tried navigating that avenue when I was *in prison* – but got ordered to 'scrub it'.

And I still think it ends 'Love ever'….

Ministry of Justice

Jeremy Wright MP
Parliamentary Under-Secretary of
State for Justice
102 Petty France
London SW1H 9AJ

T
F
E

www.justice.gov.uk

 MP
Labour Party

Our ref: 347716   13th August 2013

Dear

SHANNON TRUST READING SCHEME

Thank you for your office's e-mail of 6 August, referencing correspondence from your constituent Mr Robinson, in which he expresses an interest in attending the launch of the Shannon Trust's reading scheme.

The launch is principally to promote within public sector prisons the incorporation of the reading scheme in the 'benchmarks'. The benchmarking project is part of a large scale programme of changes to deliver further efficiencies and improvements. As such, the officials who are making arrangements for the launch are focusing attention on the good practice which already exists within some prisons and few if any invitations to attend the event will be issued. It is not therefore an event to which members of the public generally would be invited.

If your constituent's interest in attending was motivated by a desire to become involved in the wider roll-out of the scheme, then I suggest he contacts the Shannon Trust and enquires about becoming a volunteer.

I enclose a copy of this response for you to send on to your constituent should you wish.

Yours ever

Jeremy

JEREMY WRIGHT

Checking In

Part of the agenda for prison reform is saying yes to anyone who will listen to you, which is how I found myself in Leicester over an August bank-holiday weekend booked for both a radio show and an overnight stay in one of Adrian Mole's locale's hotels.

Believe it or not, talking for sixty minutes whilst concentrating like mad is exceptionally hard work – so is fighting for prison reform, come to that. Much harder work than any toils I completed in prison – so I was more than ready for some R&R when I presented myself to a receptionist – Dutch – to check in at my Mole hole.

Positioning myself at the desk another gentleman, I assume attempting the same task as me, or perhaps already a guest, shuffled up behind me and politely waited for our capable Hostess from Holland to complete the procedure of housing me.

He was just a bloke in the queue.

I told this young lady my name – and that I had a reservation. She looked me in the eye – and then eyeballed the gentleman behind me. *Right* behind me. Her line – having obviously put two and two together and concluded five: "A double room sir?" I nodded assent and her eyes went back to the gentleman behind me…

The most enormous penny dropped deep within me that this young lady thought my new friend and I were in close harmony checking in together – and were perhaps *very* good friends. I didn't know *what* to say. I don't give a toss about people's sexuality but it was more than clear that I had been temporarily earmarked for a team I most certainly do not play for. The formalities for checking-in were done with lightning haste and it was only when I got my key card – and departed the scene solo, did it become airily apparent to her that the other fella was not with me and had an independent query.

Each time I saw this young lady for the rest of my stay I was obliged ad nauseam to smile at her in the most macho way possible, a lucid ploy to reinforce my manhood, vying to prove the philosophy of my preferred state of play – genre wise – in the manifestations of the bedroom department. She probably thought I was demented.

The return leg down-south the following day took me to HMP Bedford for a pre-arranged meeting. By that I mean near it, not in it, if you get my drift. Kick-off for that one was 1830 and having arrived at the grim location the car was parked in a residential street right next to the prison walls at 1800.

I have been back to HMP Bedford since my departure from the premises a couple of times. Once was for some newspaper thing – another to meet an MP. On both occasions I walked around the entire establishment – feeling peculiar. Those gargantuan walls are *high*.

And *my* behaviour had placed me the *other side* of them…

This time I didn't take the tour but instead leant against the car smoking a cigarette. Some internal calendar calculations took place…

August bank holiday-weekend…

Good Lord. It was this bank-holiday when I was supposed to move to Hollesley Bay but didn't. More importantly, it was this damn three day event that I had to endure with Albert Steptoe… As this kicked around my head I became aware of some noise… shouting… disturbance… Realisation set in. I could hear the *Window Warriors…*

And it was only quarter past six.

I am not going to go anywhere near breaching with my feeble pen how hearing those voices from the windows of Bedford jail brought back such shuddering memories.

My appointment was near the main entrance of the prison so hugging the walls – round I went. I was not the only thing to arrive at this point for up-rolled a prison van – referred in the trade as a sweatbox. After the sound-effects reminder of my time in Bedford I now got a visual wake-up call on how prisoners are transported. This brought more memories flooding back. Rooted to the spot I witnessed this thing pull-up to the main prison doors and await admission. The last time such an event had happened here involving me, I had been aboard, looking out of the window in absolute terror.

The door teasingly slowly opened. From the other side of the road I studied the now revealed interior of the airlock system that our prisons have. There was that damn wall again – the one with no paint on it.

The vehicle edged slowly in. Once fully contained, as if by magic, the door started to close behind it – removing from my vision that dreaded mortar. I wondered how many people were aboard – as they 'checked-in' to HMP Bedford.

And I wonder by the time you read this – how many of them will have come out – only at some point to return again. The reoffending of prisoners at its apogee.

Rod Redemption (Part Six)

Having not heard from Rod for a bit – a text was discharged – checking up on him I suppose. He didn't respond for quite a few days. When I eventually heard back he rationalised that work had been relentless and he was exhausted. Encouragement was cast back his way. A reminder to behave himself was poked and laughing, he protested that he didn't have time to do anything other than toil.

Things were looking good. I asked how he was getting on with his probation officer and offered to come with him on some future appointment to demonstrate support.

He said he'd speak to them on the subject on his next visit.

House of Cards

Frances Urquhart is alive and well. More of that later. On that subject though, I have learnt a lot about how the world of Westminster operates during my battles to get various absurd events logged during my imprisonment resolved. The writers of *Yes Minister* have a new apprentice. No wonder it was Margaret Thatcher's favourite program on the telly.

Politicians speak an exclusive Urquhart language. They won't answer questions that they don't want to. The suits focus on what suits them – and they tailor hemline headlines to their taste. They ignore what doesn't float their boat and some… don't do what they say they're going to do. As well as their bespoke method of communication, they also have the most amazing way of not committing to anything that could involve ramifications.

There is little, if any, off the peg, out of the box couture in their culture. Argumentum: a recent telephone call with one such Urquhart clone – whom I had previously had a meeting with. I'll jump in mid-conversation…

JR

The prison Minister is announcing something big next month about Toe by Toe.

URQUHART

Good for you.

JR

I have no idea if this is because of anything I've done. I hope you know that I've not been doing this for me. I just want prison to make sense. Clap people into jug but give them leadership. Some of them could be huge successes.

URQUHART

Jonathan, your name is knocking about like mad at the MoJ and NOMS. The book's causing a hell of a stir. It's ruffled them.

JR

Good. I want prisoners to be given the chance to turn their lives around. You know, I've asked a lot of members of the public during all this what they want from the wayward prison system. They get to choose either answer 'A' or answer 'B'. I asked some young girl in a coffee bar last week – she was 21 – and option 'A' was bread and water, you know, breaking rocks and option 'B' was hard work, leadership, reward when it was due and stopping the revolving door. She chose option 'B'.

URQUHART

I'd have 'em all on bread and water.

JR

Come of it. No one has said I'm wrong. Everyone has said I am spot on. No one has said it's bollocks. The only lot who can't admit I'm right are your lot. I have only had "bang on Jonathan" or "no comment." And the "no comment" is always your mob. NO ONE has said I'm talking crap. Surely you agree with me?

URQUHART

No comment.

As a footnote to this, before the call ended – with assurances from both parties that everyone would be kept in the loop, I asked him if indeed one day, he wanted to be Prime Minister. Urquhart's answer was a touch ironic: "Not bloody likely. I want to write books."

Rod Redemption (Part Seven)

More radio silence made me twitchy. A check-up text was despatched which was unanswered. Plan B came and went with me leaving him a voicemail message. Nothing. Plan C was executed via an SOS to probation peeps, making it clear I was more than worried.

Never Wrong

Nowadays as our country's leaders stagger supremely on, get one to admit an error and I'll show you hen's teeth. It seems it's acceptable to admit a boo-boo when one is no longer in office – a Home Secretary of days past has recently – as I write – shamefully admitted that the then government may have got the anticipated numbers of immigrants to the UK a tad wrong. A tad? I am the only person on my street who speaks English.

OK, some artistic licence there, but you get the point.

Inability to admit fault – it appears to me – is just beyond a politician's DNA. The ancient Greeks knew a thing or two about holding their hands up; Sophocles: *"All men may err; but he that keepeth not his folly, but repenteth, doeth well; but stubbornness cometh to great trouble"*. I may suggest that someone with a paint brush gets busy daubing that on the loo walls at Westminster – I have met more *prisoners* willing to admit wrongdoing than politicians.

Case in point – the existing government recently announced that newcomers to these shores must be proficient in the language that we speak before we start financially entertaining them. If you're a newbie, in order to get housing, medical, free education for your kids or unemployment benefit, you are going to be invited to learn the language of your new home before state pound notes come your way for being on the estate. Makes sense I suppose.

And so too it does when MP's of the government's persuasion make appreciative noises to what their glorious leaders have proclaimed. A news-bite here, a social media wolf-whistle there. It all helps to say we are doing a top-notch job chaps and I think it's just jolly super.

It was rather amusing then – to this individual – when one such MP broadcast his thoughts on newly-landed incumbents being made to learn the Queen's English before they started receiving bits of paper that originate from the Royal Mint. Trouble is, this zealous MP made a – wait for it – mistake – in his public support of Number 10. I replied to his message inquiring if he had learnt to read at HMP Hollesley Bay.

Instead of him laughing it off and seeing the funny side of things, MP mode kicked-in and he deleted his original quote.

The trouble is – for him – is that I had already taken a photograph of it.

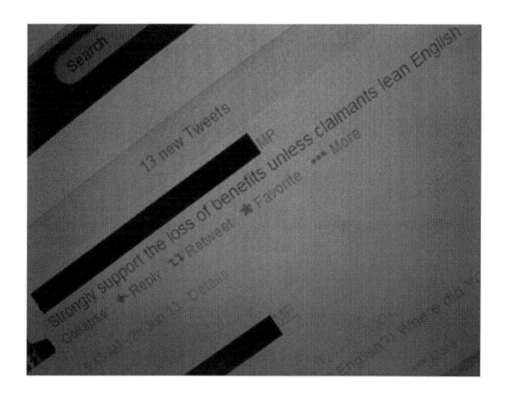

Monty

(Field Marshal Bernard Montgomery)

"Decisions! And a general, a commander in chief who has not got the quality of decision, then he is no good."

9.10

Life is funny. Cyclical. What goes around comes around.

I'm writing this on September 10th 2013 (1051) wondering what is actually going to happen tomorrow. Will the Prison Minister *really* announce that Toe by Toe is to become mandatory – a dynamic no-brainer decision if that is the case...

Has any of the door beating been of consequence? No matter – the conduit of the result is irrelevant – but the outcome crucial.

Strangely, I've just had message through one of the social media sites that I have been waging my war through. It made me stop and think – after all it was pretty much the same question that I fired-off to Jeffrey Archer all those months ago asking for guidance...

I'm typing up the last twenty pages of my six year prison experience. All written in hand! Do you know any publishers?

Sounds familiar doesn't it? I responded with exactly the same advice that I had received; have a gander at the *Writers' and Artists' Yearbook*. Who knows? Maybe another prison book is on the horizon...

The initial writing of IN IT – during prison – was undoubtedly self-distraction to my self-destruction. A port in my personal storm. My Tom, Dick and Harry. Sugar to help the pill down with. Scribbling down everything that happened and then rewriting those hasty notes every evening – twice, one for export, the second as 'back-up' – more than occupied my time. I am not sure the Ministry of Justice are too over the moon about the end result. However if the system had given me more work to do, I would have had less time to write.

Perhaps I could have spent my time teaching prisoners to read...

Prison for me was *so* one-dimensional. Yet those within were *multi-dimensioned*. But the system – *no* scope, *no* depth – shuns the talent. Jesus – I had *Statham* and *Moyles* characters – why on earth not *do something* with them? As the management warehoused – I scribed.

Relentlessly.

I would have given anything to film what happened – not possible of course – but Lord was the *talent* there. And believe me, some of the absurdities felt like a film.

They never made *Carry on Prison*...

Ministry of Justice Productions Ltd

C A L L   S H E E T

IN IT

Day 116.   Thursday, November 10th, 2011.   Scenes 97, 89A, 74C, 110, 111 & 112.
"Healthcare" "Bricks" "Wilford" Unit.

ARTISTE	CHARACTER	HAIR AND MAKE UP
Mr Jonathan Robinson	BIGGLES/BASIL FAWLTY	0630
Mr Jason Statham	ROD	0630
Mr Philip Seymour Hoffman	NURSE PHILIP	0630
Miss Kathy Bates	WELSH DRAGON	0630

Extras: Prisoners, Prison officers, Civilian office staff. (Extras on set 0815 please - except Wilford Residents who can't work until 1130) N.B. Animal team to keep all dogs away from Wilford Unit to stop them passing out again. Education Department is stood down. (For entire production following Head of Education's orders.

WARDROBE:	AS PREVIOUS. PLEASE CHECK WITH CONTINUITY.
MAKE UP:	MR ROBINSON'S HAIR TO BE GREYED UP.
PROPS:	NEWSPAPERS. IT APPEARS THAT THE THREE TRUCK LOADS THAT ARRIVE EACH DAY ARE NOT ENOUGH. CAN PROPS PLEASE ENSURE THAT PRISON OFFICER ARTISTES ARE ONLY ISSUED ONE PER DAY.
TRANSPORT:	ARTISTES TO ARRIVE ON FOOT. CREW ARRIVING BY CAR ARE ADVISED NOT TO LEAVE EXPENSIVE BELONGINGS IN VIEW. THE THIRD ASSISTANT DIRECTOR'S ALLOY WHEELS ARE STILL BEING SEARCHED FOR.
CATERING:	FRENCH STICKS.
SECURITY:	THE UNIT'S SECURITY COMPANY HAS LEFT THE PRODUCTION FOLLOWING PROTECTION MONEY THREATS FROM COSFORD UNIT. SECURITY IS NOW BEING PROVIDED BY BASHER MCENZIE OF STOW UNIT.
SOUND EFFECTS:	TO BE PROVIDED BY THE WINDOW WARRIORS OF HMP BEDFORD.
STUNTS:	FIRE BREATHERS ON STAND-BY FOR MS. BATES' CLOSE UP.
SFX:	FOG MACHINE FOR WILFORD'S CORRIDORS.
COMMUNICATIONS:	MOBILE PHONE RECEPTION SEEMS BEST AROUND "BOSNIA" UNIT.

The writing of ON IT has been altogether a different kettle of fish to what was penned in clink. Somewhere in the back of my mind since IN IT was released – and during my campaign to get prisoners teaching other prisoners to read – and the barring of that process to be criminalised – I wish – I always wondered if there was another story to be told. I'll leave it to you Dear Reader to pass judgement on that but I will comment on how this malarkey has been penned – which has utilised a completely different process to that which was written in clink. After all, everything before you now has been scribed sometime after the events depicted occurred.

'Writing is all about re-writing' said Dick Clement and for sure I have played around considerably with what you have nearly trawled through. Whilst I'm on that subject – thank you for doing so. Writing for me is enjoyable (Christ I hope reading my rubbish is alright) and highly therapeutic. It's also bloody hard work. I've been asked a lot recently how I go about it – so here's some behind the scenes 'DVD extras' for you. If you're an aspiring writer – I hope it helps.

Wrongly or rightly I see writing as a very similar process to film making; a cumulative effort – shame the prison system isn't. A script is written, the cast and crew hired, the material's shot, edited and hey presto. BUT – you need a *lot* of money to do it. I sort of write the same way but it's cheaper and I haven't had to pay Penelope Cruz's wages.

Down on the page *everything* goes but for me, the actual *shooting* is the *re-writes*. Your first manuscript is your *shooting-script*. If something can be better, whether it's a cut, an addition – just 'film' that piece again. A re-take. And do as many re-takes as you like. If you're a writer – *you* are the director. Joanna Trollope encouraged us all in prison to give writing a go. I suggest the same to you.

If this idiot can do it – anyone can at least give it a shot.

J K Rowling better not be reading this.

9.11

Dear Mr Wright,

Following consultation with _____'s office further to your letter to him of August 15th we concluded that it was best I responded to you. This after I was initially advised to email _____@justice.gsi.gov.uk for confirmation of my attendance at today's MoJ/Shannon Trust announcement.

I did send an email to that address. I have yet to receive a response.

I am aware Mr Grayling first put me on your radar in January of this year when he kindly responded to my email alerting me that he had forwarded my epistle on to you. Assuming that the Kremlin communication system is slightly more efficient than the HMP bush telegraph – not difficult – I hope you are also aware that I met with MOJ personage on March 15th following the reading of my book down

Petty France way.

During that meeting one of the questions put to me was: *Why doesn't prison work?*

After I had orally repeated things already logged within IN IT such as officers asleep on duty, the complete lack of passion, a gaping hole of leadership and the many wasted opportunities witnessed by this idiot during a more than fully deserved prison sentence I posed what the MoJ was going to do about the barring of Toe by Toe by the __ Head of Education, a Mr _____ _____ at HMP Hollesley Bay on September 1st, 2011.

His response: *The MoJ cannot comment on a specific incident.*

At this point in my letter I would like to draw your attention to transcripts of this year from the House of Commons. Firstly, from Thursday May 9th and a quote from Chris Grayling: *I want to see those prisoners who can read teaching those who cannot to do so.*

The second from July 2nd and rhetoric from yourself: *I agree with my hon. Friend. He is right to cite the Shannon Trust. Its Toe by Toe project is an extremely good example of what we are discussing. We will help it in any way we can.*

You were then asked if you were supportive of such schemes – and if you <u>were aware of</u> <u>any barriers they might have met</u>. I have studied your response and whilst you appear to acknowledge it as a worthy process – you did not, in my view, answer the second part of the question.

The reason I wished to attend today's announcement is twofold. Firstly, I am *delighted* that at *last*, the Shannon Trust's Toe by Toe reading plan is to get more credibility within the system and secondly I wanted to ask you personally if you were aware of any past barriers the scheme had been blockaded by and what your intentions were to deal with them.

On my release on HDC in November of 2011 about the first people I rang were the Shannon Trust. They listened to my version of events of September 1st.

I have subsequently learnt from other parties that my experiences are by *no* means unique.

During the promotion of IN IT, my campaign – which incidentally has been *completely independent* of any Trust, charity or organisation, my primary focus has been to plea for a cessation of the in-house shooting-down of rehabilitation/peer-to-peer mentoring that I now know is an everyday occurrence within our prisons. I don't know if you have read my book – but *heavens*, is the system <u>missing a trick</u> on exploiting the potential of *some* prisoners – and my orders from a company that the MoJ are paying £7,751,340,00 to "scrub Toe by Toe" came my way in an *open resettlement* prison.

With all that income, I presume they have lawyers to hand who would have sued me in a more than lively manner if I spoke or for that matter wrote, with forked tongue.

I therefore respectfully ask that you respond to my letter and cover each point. Your closing comment in your communication to _____ that I volunteer my services to the Shannon Trust is the catalyst for my campaign. I tried taking that route once before…

_____ ordered me to stop.

I look forward to your reply.

Yours Sincerely,

Jonathan Robinson.

(Author: Mr Wright never responded to this letter. Read into that what you will).

Teevee (Part Two)

So many events in this volume start with an inbound phone call. This one – around Toe by Toe lift-off time – joins the ranks. An unfamiliar but not hidden mobile number got my attention. "Jonathan?" The voice was familiar – and it was only on, or near about, the third 'innit' that the penny dropped…

Teevee.

Full of beans as ever – probably wondering when the next meal was coming his way, or knowing him, what time *Eastenders* or *Corrie* was on – and with stupendous news, for during this phone call I learnt that Teevee was out of prison – and had been for some time, was working on the straight and narrow and above all else – not that those two prefaces are lacking vitality – had just become a father. I was thrilled for him. A little girl.

A portable Teevee.

Victory

The Guardian

Monday 16 September 2013

A pioneering prison literacy scheme, which began with correspondence between a Sussex farmer and a life sentence prisoner, is to be officially delivered across the penal estate after ministers recognised its potential to change prisoner lives and cut reoffending.

The charity, Shannon Trust, was started in 1997 after farmer Christopher Morgan, published a book containing letters between him and Tom Shannon, a life sentence prisoner. Morgan had been shocked to learn of the low levels of literacy in the prison population and devoted the royalties from the book, Invisible Crying Tree to setting up peer mentoring reading schemes in prisons.

The Trust's first 'prisoners-teaching-prisoners' to read programme began in Wandsworth prison in 2001, facilitated by prison officer Neil Lodge. It proved a success and, within 18 months, was operating in 30 jails. The Trust's peer teaching approach is now running in 150 jails. At least 10,000 prisoners have been taught to read through the programme.

It is estimated almost half of the prison population has a reading age at, or below, that of a child of 11. Talking about the Shannon reading plan last year, Nick Hardwick, chief inspector of prisons, said: "At a time when politicians and policy makers are looking to break the cycle of reoffending, here is something we know works."

The Trust will now deliver the programme in every public sector prison in England and Wales, after being appointed as a business partner by the National Offender Management Service (NOMS).

Prisons minister Jeremy Wright, who last week announced the partnership at Wandsworth jail, said the reading scheme would be rolled out across every public prison in England and Wales and, wherever a prisoner goes, access to the scheme will follow.

He said the ability to read can change lives and believes new found literacy will have an impact on reoffending. He had particular praise for the prisoner mentors, who were at the launch, and said he plans to encourage them to take their mentoring skills out into the community.

'John' is a mentor at Wandsworth. He said teaching fellow prisoners to read was the most rewarding thing he had ever done: "I get such a buzz when a learner completes a page for the first time, it is just so exciting".

Until now, the success of the Shannon scheme has depended on the goodwill of individual prison governors and officers. Now, it will become part of the 'core day' in every public prison.

The chief executive of Shannon Trust says this will give the Trust unprecedented access to many thousands of prisoners who cannot read.

"Thousands of literate prisoners would like to use their time in prison positively by teaching other prisoners to read. Our partnership with NOMS gives us the ability to release this potential and make a radical difference to literacy levels across all prisons".

Where Credit's Due

18 September 2013

Without doubt the worst is always feared when I enter a prison. One week after the Ministry of Justice (rather hushed) announcement of Toe by Toe becoming mandatory in all our jails I found myself in HMP Brixton. As a guest – of the non-staying variety. Back along the Ballad of Reading Gaol cavernous corridors labyrinth I travelled. Through those gloomy internal airlock steel gates. The conveyor belt walking time machine again. Hollowly echoes of inaugural arrival at HMP Bedford sounded the division bell. One security junction formality was concluded outside a building – inside the prison – and as I waited my turn a fence was leant on. Skyscraper high it was. *That* wire again.

The brick backdrop view was taken in. Those period-trapping walls again. Flashbacks came vividly back. Despite being in central London, I suppose the inside of one jail looks like any other. Like last time in prison situ, my immediate penitentiary environment was surveyed.

Tunnels were everywhere.

That is no pun. Building work was taking place at ground-level around the estate and regimented race-track lanes of newly laid tarmac surfaced the deck like sinewy spilt spaghetti. Another member of the visiting ensemble remarked about 'all the tunnels' as I peered into a terra firma black hole wondering if a muddy tunnel-man was about to emerge having fallen short. He didn't.

Once finally in – about 150 of us – we got down to the business in hand. A seminar on education in jail and the challenges facing the establishment on keeping people out of prison. My expectation was glum. I was proved wrong. The atmosphere was dynamite. Nothing like the pedestrian affair that was the serene desolation of barren-limbo anaemic Hollesley Bay.

Having anticipated gloomy crevice warehousing I learnt that Brixton had set-up a Cat D wing and 90 – count 'em – suitably assessed inmates were leaving the establishment each day to go to work. And they were coming back. No contest that Hollesley Bay was exporting a workforce on a daily basis but the feeling in this place was just *different*. There was soul in the remit. Interest. Passion. The inmates even called the main Governor by his Christian name – an unusual spectacle from my past perspective – I never even *met* the Admiral of my two sinking ships…

Cards on table: I was impressed. OK there was probably a fair amount of set-dressing that had gone on but I had my prisoner ears on. And my prisoner eyes open. The MoJ could benefit by getting some other prison proprietors to have a sniff around HMP Brixton, to see how things *can* be done. Full credit to the Governor there. I had a chat with him…

The poor devil looked wide eyed as Basil Fawlty leapt on him. On learning that I was the fella who had written the book he thought I was a staff member (!) so quick correct identification was volunteered forthwith. I hope by the time this gets published his eyebrows have returned to closer proximity to his ocular organs because they skyrocketed pretty sharpish. Once essential elements of my motivations had been communicated he said – a little defensively – that Toe by Toe was up and running in his prison. I asked him if he had heard word from the hierarchy that it was henceforth mandatory – as I had learned that the Kremlin wanted to instruct all Governors personally of the news before admitting publically that they had put the reading plan into the remit – and seven days had ticked away since the prison Minister's announcement. Plenty of time to bang out an email, write a letter or pick up the telephone…

"No, I haven't heard anything."

The seminar was indisputably good. Prisoners spoke, the Governor spoke, the Chaplain spoke and then the Ministry of Justice Deputy Director of the Rehabilitation Programme – a lady – fluidly said her piece. Familiar stuff – as full-bodied diverting as ever: Education is important, rehabilitation is important, resettlement is important… I'm sure you get the idea…

She asked if anyone had any questions…

I was on my nonconformist feet as if I'd been electrocuted. A microphone was placed in my mitt. As per the norm in jail my voice probably gave her no indication as to what was coming her way. Here's – give or take – the dialogue:

JR

You've said that education is important in rehabilitation. Do you agree that teaching illiterate prisoners to read is vital to this cause?

MoJ

Yes. Absolutely. Very Important.

JR

And do you agree that peer mentoring – and positive encouragement from staff – as we have heard here this evening, can only be seen as a positive way forward?

MoJ

For sure. The work here is tremendous.

JR

Can you explain to me then why when I was in jail (CUE GASPS FROM AUDIENCE) *I was barred from teaching Toe by Toe – a peer mentoring reading plan – that last week the prison Minister announced at HMP Wandsworth is to become mandatory, in an open resettlement prison by a company that you pay more than seven and a half million pounds to provide prison education services to?*
(STUNNED HUSH FROM AUDIENCE)

MoJ

(Reaching for smelling salts) *Er…. Um…. Er….. Can we talk in private afterwards?*

We did indeed talk privately afterwards. But not before various people came up to me and asked if that had really happened. I found myself telling the gathering clamouring crowd exactly what had gone down at Hollesley Bay – or not – and was met with sentiments expressed – among others – of: *unbelievable, disgusting, absurd* and *a monstrous wrong*. I wrote them down. That's what I do when I'm in prison, innit.

Once the spirit of Hartshorne had aroused our MoJ lady back into consciousness she asked me to tell all. I did – and told her of past correspondence/meetings with her colleagues and divulged names. Her lips were very thin at this point. It was agreed that the best way forward was to take all my details – she would look into all of the utterly ridiculous events and categorically, without fail, she *assured* me she would be back in touch with me.

I am writing this particular section of the masterpiece that is ON IT nearly two months since that conversation.

I have heard nothing.

Rod Redemption (Part Eight)

Not a dicky bird heard from Statham. Another text was sent which was not replied to so I dug out a number of someone I had liaised with whilst Rod was in prison. I spoke to this individual who told me that he was alive and still working. I asked for a message to get through to him to contact me.

The silence had surprised me – but we all deal with the post-prison experience in different ways. Indeed, some cast members of IN IT who had declared undying ambition to stay in touch hadn't even squeaked.

It's a funny old world.

The Crown Prosecution Service

26 September 2013

Nine charged over fraud

Following an investigation by the Thames Valley Police Economic Crime Unit, the CPS has authorised charges against six women and three men in connection with alleged fraudulent activity at_____ (___), a social purpose company contracted by the Department of Work and Pensions (DWP) to deliver the '___ _____' employment and training scheme.

It is alleged that between February 2009 and February 2013 nine___ employees including one contract manager, seven recruiters and an administrator, employed across three___ offices in the South East of England, committed numerous offences of fraud. It is alleged that they forged documentation to support fraudulent claims to the DWP for reward payments which, under the terms of the contract, were paid out when the scheme successfully placed individuals in employment. It is alleged that many of the reward payments related either to people who never attended ____ or to clients whom ____ had not successfully placed in employment. The contract was to deliver motivation and training and to assist people to find employment.

The nine individuals are charged with a total of 60 offences, including conspiracy to defraud, multiple counts of forgery, and making and possessing articles for use in fraud.

Ofsted

10 October 2013

"65% of education and training in prisons is not good enough"

The National Director for Further Education and Skills, Matthew Coffey: It is unacceptable that not one prison has been rated outstanding for education in the past four years and only one in three is rated good. If the figures related to schools there would be a national outcry.

Education Provider's Website (Part Two)

The Offender Learning and Skills Service (OLASS)

"As the largest independent provider of education in prisons, we've delivered OLASS since 2005, providing over 1.5 million hours of learning and vocational training. We currently employ over 1,000 staff to deliver courses that range from basic literacy to the arts."

Sir Sean Connery (Part Two)

"Memories of working with people who are fun, industrious, talented and enthusiastic. These are all the qualities that I find admirable. The rest of you – well you know who you are…"

Media Mayhem

Whenever a jail related story breaks-out various media mediums launch distress flares appealing for ex-prisoners to present themselves for interview. One such day four appointments were made with a bunch of broadcasters to grill this particular member of the club. A morning conversation took place on air with me locked alone in some broom cupboard in the bowels of my local radio station talking to an interviewer down the line from a national network. This was beyond strange. I prefer having someone the other side of the buttons to see and talk to so conversing with a wall – knowing the whole country had audible access to my rubbish – was bizarre. Fortunately it went without hitch and instructions were passed to return in the late afternoon for more – one of them a TV piece – all worryingly close together on the timing front.

During the interlude telephone calls came and went from frantic front-line studio directors alerting me of times, what we were going to talk about and general media hokum. I smiled sweetly down the phone announcing my intentions to comply and not bump into the furniture. They thanked me for my 'professionalism' (?) and revealed that I would be given assistance to guide me through the hoops from studio to studio as the remaining spots were on the trot and more than tightly articulated on the schedule.

I was to ask for Dillon.

In accordance I presented myself punctually pre the appointed hour and found him. From the outset, things did not look good. He wore sandals, had a wet fish handshake and looked like he was on his way to a *Magic Roundabout* fan convention. An appalling cup of coffee – it was worse than convict caffeine – was accepted as Dillon attached various wires to me. Having been plonked into a chair in front of a camera with a busy chattering newsroom behind me I looked like I was on a life support machine. Dillon seemed *very* relaxed. One of the lengthy lifeline cables stuffed down my collar was an earpiece which bleeped alarmingly loudly.

In hindsight – this was the warning signal that things were not going to go as planned.

With about five minutes to go before being patched into the main network – and a well-known news presenter who had earlier that day through social media promoted that he would be talking to me, Dillon was told that all I could hear was ear-splitting beeps. He started to fiddle with some dials. This made the beeps worse. Dillon now looked slightly less relaxed. A lady appeared – I just made out over the noisy newshounds and the electronic racket that she was going to whisk me off to the next studio for the following radio interview once the television spot was done. Speed, she indicated, would be of essence.

Still the beeps blipped. Dillon, looking mystified, twirled some more dials and switches. As the crucial minutes ticked away his relaxed demeanour gradually dismantled, drastically switching from folk-town hippy to someone who'd been asked to disarm an atomic bomb. The time-keeping lady kept looking at her watch.

The beeping continued.

Dillon called for reporter reinforcements.

Two volunteered themselves. One held a polystyrene cup, the other a Mars Bar.

As the cup bearing member of the rescue party rummaged about around my knees checking the wires, the chocolate chewer had a go at the Space Shuttle cockpit quantity of buttons – I even had a go. Switches were thrown backwards and forwards, dials were turned in all directions yet still the beeping continued. The lady with the watch – now ashen faced – continued to consult her time bomb ticking warhead timepiece. Dillon had beads of sweat glowing as he tried everything and anything on the Dr Frankenstein selection of knobs and levers. The polystyrene chap at my feet cursed and swore like a man possessed. The chit-chat from the newsroom rumble garbled merrily on. I sat in my chair with more wires attached to me than the *Six Million Dollar Man* in theatre.

Somehow – Dillon pressed *something* that worked as on top of the beeps there was a hint of a male voice instructing me to wave at the camera if I could hear him. I waved like an unaccompanied debutante at a dance and told the lens I could only just make their voice out. Still with one cup-clamping chap on his knees in front of me and Dillon looking plain confused, a female voice could now – just – be heard over the relentless beeps and the volcanic volume of conversation erupting from the Fleet Street festivities behind me. I told the lens I couldn't hear her over the stertorous lava.

"Tell them to fucking shut up," *screamed* the voice. "Um…Er…" said I, rotating my chair. "The lady in my ear is asking if you could hold the conversation down a wee bit."

About seven well blooded hacks looked at me as if I had asked them to strip naked. They stopped conversing for five seconds, then resumed – with gusto. *"TELL THEM TO FUCKING SHUT UP!"* yelled the earpiece over the beeps as Alvar Lidell turned in his grave. "Um, I did," I said to the lens. Time-keeping lady stared at her watch. I stared at the lens. Dillon stared at the ceiling.

Then a phone rang.

Dillon – now fountain perspiring, shakily answered it. "It's for you," he said passing me the phone. Still manacled to my chair with enough wiring to loom a 737 the receiver was placed to my non-pulsing ear. "I'm sorry Jonathan, it's a foul-up and we've missed your spot. Can we do this another time?" Acknowledgment of this news was passed both to the caller and to she-with-the-watch. With no hesitation her response was to start grabbing at wires with Houdini haste to release me. We had, she puffed, about a minute to be on the other side of the building for the next scheduled radio spot.

Three seizures later – with cables dangling out of all parts of my clothes – we made it last-minute to the morning's broom cupboard and I told the wall again of all the rehabilitation not going on in our prisons. Wall had heard this story earlier but didn't react to hearing the same fable again.

Bricks and mortar conversation complete, off to the final studio we waltzed, still whilst wires were whipped away.

The final broadcast of the day went fine. It is strange telling the same story over and over. Somewhere deep down part of my brain was telling me I was repeating myself but that got blanked. This was a different audience. A different network. This isn't wall. Shut up and get on with it. And so I did.

And so I will keep doing.

Action Is Eloquence

Most British governments – *terrified* of the prison issue – would, if they had Ridley Scott technology probably jump – nay, *leap* – at the chance of transporting their prisoners off to some distant planet – a lunar convict colony – and focus its primary rhetoric on subject matters that they believe the public want to hear so they can be re-elected come polling day. Discuss – or try to – matters prison with a politician – *any* politician – and you'll see a head buried in the sand with tempo that would make an ostrich envious.

In early *Blackadder* days Britain didn't quite know what to do with its criminals. If one transgressed the law it was highly likely a ticket – one way – to some far-off land would be on the itinerary. The passage – if it was survived – was in 'Chain Class', one below what became the blueprint for future budget airlines. This cosseting-the-problem-under- the-rug of what-do-we-do-with-our-convicts came to an end when the likes of Australia – now armed with Ned Kelly, a by-product of transportation – declared that Great Britain could keep its own wrong 'uns thank you very much. After some head scratching in Westminster, a debate or two and some hefty luncheons – and as rockets had not yet been invented – disappointingly cons couldn't be corralled on planet Pluto – the then government concentrated on its home-based prison system. Let's put all these ghastly people away somewhere then the problem will disappear and we can all look the other way.

Oh dear.

Somewhere down the line, in Queen Victoria's era I believe, some bright spark in a suit deduced that if something wasn't done to *rehabilitate* prisoners whilst they were guests of Vicky and Albert they would keep coming back to clink. An early revolving door had been flagged. Repeat business was high. Additionally, it was costing a *fortune*. What to do?

Many years later Westminster suits (takers of the *Times*) quietly ordered the admin suits (*Guardian*) to do some research. The admin allsorts got the clipboard department (*Independent*) to look into the clientele (*Sun*) behind-the-door where – surprise, surprise – it was clocked that an awful lot of the non-paying guests were illiterate. What hope was there that on release Magwitch could get a job and go straight if he or she *couldn't read*? The clipboard bearers reported back to the admin collective who delivered due diligence to the Westminster mob. Very quietly.

The government quivered the quandary. So too did successive governments. And governments after that mulled too. Ostrich heads sank to the sand everywhere. Westminster whispered that it couldn't be seen to be educating these awful people. The voters would go mad. We won't get re-elected. For now parliament was *very* conscious of public reaction. For lo, someone had invented the *Daily Mail.*

Orders from on-high habitually instructed MP's to kiss babies, appear on breakfast television, *try* not to accept money in brown envelopes for appearing in reality TV programs shot in lands where we used to send our criminals, attempt to go-green – *cycle* to and from Downing Street but DO NOT swear at Policemen and above all else – do NOT talk prison politics.

The Kremlin decreed that they would allow some troublesome charities to bubble in the background and occasionally sound-off when something kicked-off within those walls. They even allowed some lot called the Shannon Trust – who practiced some new-fangled reading scheme called Toe by Toe – to sporadically operate behind enemy lines, popping their heads up above the parapet in a guerrilla warfare campaign parachuting-in instructors among staff who, when not asleep on duty or glued to tabloid newspapers (*Sport*), merrily mirrored a stokers' reunion. Worse; barriers from private education providers who are paid more than £7.6M had to be circumnavigated.

Not always successfully.

These providers don't do a bundle over the pesky Shannon Trust, for their scheme involves volunteers (shudder; no charge) training enthusiastic convicts who *can* read to mentor their colleagues who can't via the Toe by Toe method which is – shock horror; free. A major fly in the providers' ointment come renegotiation time for big juicy contracts. *Ker-ching,* the onomatopoeia goes. And so too up-in-smoke wisps away the opportunity to do something <u>positive</u> whilst doing time. The Shannon Trust's plea on the Prison Reform Trust's website: *"There is this huge swathe of people in prison who we could be helping that we are not."*

The prison population is a diverse one. Leading the percentage of inhabitants – from this idiot's experience – is a group absorbed with the manufacture and distribution of funny looking cigarettes. Other actions to get incarcerated are available too. Most people in prison are uneducated, have mental health issues and, as one member of the probation service once said to me, are damaged goods. The numbers in prison tally some 85,000. More than three-quarters of them cannot read, write or count to the standard expected of an 11-year-old. The incredulity of Lord Ramsbotham at the system not fixing this curable cancer whilst personage are playing *Porridge* is much cited, so I will quote him too:

"The Prison Service is required to keep securely those committed by the courts, to treat them with humanity and to help them to live useful and law-abiding lives in prison and on release.

This means using the time someone is in prison to find out why they commit crimes and doing everything possible to prevent them from committing another, by providing them with the tools needed to be a responsible member of society.

Winston Churchill realised this. Witness his words as Home Secretary on July 20, 1910, when introducing the Prison Estimates to the House of Commons:

'… A constant heart-searching by all charged with the duty of punishment… and an unfaltering faith that there is a treasure, if you can only find it, in the heart of every man – these are the symbols, which in the treatment of crime and criminals mark and measure the stored-up strength of a nation, and are the sign and proof of the living virtue in it.'

Having visited and/or inspected every prison in England, Wales and Northern Ireland as Chief Inspector, I found overcrowded, understaffed and under-resourced prisons, unable to provide every prisoner with work or education. Far too many cannot read or write and, like it or not, there is nothing for them to do from Friday afternoon to Monday morning but – locked in their cells – watch TV.

It is said there are no votes in prisons. But if voters were to ask Ministers and their MPs why the criminal justice system was failing to protect them, and witness the appallingly high reoffending rate, I suggest that could change. Ministers would be forced to address the reason why, and put right the ills that have been evident for too long."

I bet the government love *him*.

One thing that can be found in abundance in prison is camaraderie. *Unbelievable* quotas of the stuff. A classless island where providing you're a good bloke (or lass) time can be served without hassle. A shoo-in. I have never – *ever* – been surrounded by such *characters*. Some of whom – admittedly only some – would have your hand off for the chance to do something productive whilst caged. Especially if it involved something positive.

Like teaching a fellow prisoner to *read*.

Occasionally ex-prisoners release a book post experience. Mostly politicians. Or their ex-wives. Sometimes idiot helicopter pilots. These tend to either veer towards the divine discovery of religion whilst banged-up or concentrate on the priceless costs of running the damn places. All contain a degree of humour. Common ground in all the volumes focuses on the vast apathy in prison, poorly trained disinterested staff and the verging-on- criminal levels of illiteracy dans clink.

One such book concentrates on this issue rather robustly…

Meanwhile the government – to keep the *Daily Mail* off its back – and a snowball in hell's chance of being re-elected (don't get me wrong, I take the *Telegraph* but prison taught me to tell it how it is) recently sounded-off a bunch of measures to keep the electorate happy. First the new Justice Minister announced the privatisation of the probation services, then the cutting back of legal-aid before a knockout right-hook of payment by results in the future running of the CJS bandwagon. To keep the brigade content that want bread and water in the remit, smoking is going to be extinguished in prisons. So too satellite telly. Voting ain't happening either – ironic that – as the prisoners who *do* give a toss would probably vote Tory.

To some, re-jigging a system that costs a fortune – and isn't working – might make sense. Though the folk down probation way – those at the helm – have gone nothing short of mental. And it's this lot who have to deal with the masses that the prison system throws off its conveyor belt having done a whole lot of nothing with. It's strange that the cross- hairs of cost cutting have been so strongly aimed at after-sales, yet so little attention has been fired at the missed opportunity of correcting people whilst they are *in* prison. The Minister's predecessor dubbed it warehousing. He wasn't wrong.

It's odd that as the Justice Minister very publically lays into private companies charging him for tagging prisoners who are now dead – and as he drones on that he wants better value for money from his providers that he is so reluctant to address the unfathomable barring of Toe by Toe in an open resettlement prison by a company he's chucking eye-watering quantities of dosh at. This, the same company that he – when in another Ministerial role – had to dismiss as they were too great a risk. His words, not mine. The same company whose chairperson – a close czar ally of Red Square – sorry, number 10 – resigned. I suppose the hari-kari ceremonial falling on sword completed so as not to embarrass the PM. Almost unbelievably, although nothing surprises me anymore, the same company who – at the time of writing – has nine of its former employees appearing in crown court facing the music for fraud.

When the Justice Minister responded to an email of mine he included the fact that he was copying in his prison minister. This is the same individual who when interviewed on telly at the opening of one of the *Clink* restaurants – in prison eateries open to members of the public – which have been hugely successful in reducing reoffending (crikey, getting prisoners working and giving them leadership – whatever next?) instead of plying encouragement, he just sprouted stock-keep-the-*Daily-Mail*-readers-happy dialogue of "We are keeping these people locked up".

Ye Gods.

The same Minister – *very* quietly – the MoJ do like keeping their cards close to their chest – announced in September of 2013 that Toe by Toe is to become mandatory – part of the core working (?) day – in all public sector prisons. This proclamation was kept <u>so</u> off-radar that the Ministry didn't even put out a press release about it. The night before the event, their press office lackeys were unaware of it. I know. I spoke to them. The world only got word of this – super – news by the penning of the *Guardian*'s prison correspondent via their newspaper and some tall ex-prisoner bloke on a well-known social media site.

Is the Ministry of Justice that embarrassed – and so threatened by the *Daily Mail* – to admit that things could have been done better in the past? Yes methinks.

Looking forward – what is *vital* is that Toe by Toe now be allowed to run effectively and without hindrance. The full potential of those eager to get stuck-in (of which there are droves – so far; totally underutilised) must be consummately encouraged. Be of *no* doubt that there is low-lying ripe-to-pick fruit in prison. Bucket loads. Then we might, just *might*, start to see a turnaround in the dismal reoffending rates. Less of the revolving door. Maybe then, Westminster won't in the future – when Ridley Scott rockets *are* invented – have to employ the inevitable option of ostracising prisoners off to planet prison in the galaxy. For if innovative projects like Toe by Toe are not given full-fuel-boosters, the whole prison system will eventually come crashing down to earth, just like Skylab did. Most of the wreckage landed in Australia if memory serves me right.

Where we used to send our prisoners.

Rod Redemption (Part Nine)

Still a stony silence. More texts, voicemails and carrier pigeons were launched asking for contact. It was made abundantly clear that requests for communication were not in any way shape or form, any sort of attempt to chase any monies that may be owing – but just pure concern.

Round Table

17 October 2013

Two politicians and yours truly the blurb announced. A trio on the radio. The BBC had asked if I'd be interested in co-existing on-air for an hour with two Westminster suits, one Labour, the other Tory. Bears' activities in woods and the optimum religious choice of the Pope, my response. The producer asked me to tell-all with a caveat of not mentioning any prison-education providers by name. This was sufficiently agreed. I turned up fifteen minutes before transmission – I like to be fresh and not familiar with whom I'm broadcasting – such a ham – and thus three of us ended up in a green room sniffing each other out prior to sixty minutes of what I hoped would be common sense warfare on the wireless.

"Who are you?" one of them asked. On identification that I was an ex-prisoner (after they had both subconsciously patted the outside of their jackets to confirm wallet location) both of them shook my hand. They were friendly – but thrown. An engineer arrived, offered us refreshments and wheeled us into the studio. I had been on this presenter's show before and as we all traipsed in a record was playing and up our host stood and welcomed us.

Sound checks complete my eyes were resolutely glued to the red light which when illuminated – would be the green light for me to question these two on what the hell wasn't going on in our prisons on the catastrophic rehabilitation front. I, as the saying goes, was gagging for it. As the record's melody petered out, the red filament glowed and off we went.

OK, here we go, tally-ho. Jesus – there *is* still some aviator in me.

As introductions were made to listeners I was straining like a dog on a lead to get cracking. I wanted to reveal all and make these two squirm. One to relish.

Uh-uh.

First question: "Jonathan, what do you think of this country's current heating bill situation?"

Holy f___, sweet J___, crap and fried eggs internalised I, for my expertise on heating bills was such that they had to be paid – and not a lot else. *Er... Um... Hmmm. Well in this world that we live in, everyone is struggling and I know not-a-lot on this subject.*

Trying to steer the foreign matter plot-line to clink territory I pressed-ahead with *I can tell you what the heating bill is at HMP Hollesley Bay though...*

Suffice to say – the only anticipated squirming occurring was from my direction. Sixty minutes of *heating bills*? I am s*unk*. What's the next question going to be about? *Gardening*? As the two politicians sprouted out energy related statistics and numbers, within me full scale Basil Fawlty panic-stations bubbled into service.

Like a rabbit in headlights I waited for the next subject matter more than up against it. Brain was overwhelmingly mounted at pains to recollect *anything* even *remotely* stored away on Lord knows what the next topic would be. The gritting of roads? NHS costs? *The X Factor*?

Whether or not the enigmatic presenter had been toying with me I don't know – there had been a mischievous gamesmanship smirk from his direction on the launch of topic one. A rescue party galloped over the horizon with the dawn of the next subject; prison education. *Thank Christ*. The Cavalry had mercifully arrived. Flustered Fawlty within me ceased whimpering.

Out came the story with no holding back. An indisputably fully deserved prison sentence as a result of my impetuous reckless actions. The fear of my future, the very quick realisation that I was not in danger but in fact surrounded by people who needed help and encouragement during their incarceration and that my perception of those – on the whole – with keys, were fatuously inimitably lethargic and alarmingly, not terribly inclined to display much leadership.

Going for the kill, out poured the denigrated innate twisted seams events of Hollesley Bay, when I had been ordered to cancel purposeful activity via teaching illiterate adult prisoners to read – utilising an *approved* in-prison programme that the *system had trained me to tutor*, by an extraordinarily errant economics engrossed education employee, employed by a private education provider that the government was paying through the nose more than seven and a half million exultant pounds. This, I envenomed, was lunacy. It is known that teaching prisoners to read reduces reoffending and I had tried to 'do the right thing' in jail, yet a company earning a mountain of money – *voracious* for purposeful productivity on its window-dressing website – had sublimely denigrated an already top-heavy fissured system with its coffer filling franchise. The prison system is a rehabilitation lite geriatric tragicomedy refusing the look-in of a Stannah Stairlift.

I eventually shut-up and looked at the presenter – whose eyes were as dinner plates. He smilingly turned to the two politicians. Expecting political-off-the cuff waffle or robotic blandness – what omitted – from both of them – *floored* me.

"I couldn't agree with Jonathan more," said one. "Disgraceful," said the other before effectively completely verbally endorsing my campaign.

RESULT.

More of the subject matter was aired – all totally onside with my patter – and then our host as they say in the trade, went to the news. The red light went out and we were temporarily mute to the public. Off came the politicians' headphones and one of them asked me who the company was who had done this. Needless to say I told them. They both shook their heads. One said 'madness' and the other 'bananas'.

They were not referring to either the band or fresh fruit.

As the news moved to the weather and then to a traffic report, back on went the headphones before that red light lit up again. The next topic: Welfare, unemployment and the Department of Work and Pensions. I didn't care. They could have talked about parking tickets if they'd wanted to. I had got my piece over and these two had without reluctance actually backed me up. Political drawbridges had come tumbling down. The Basil within me was jumping up and down with glee.

One of them went on about the mess that the Welfare state is in – and a brainwave came my way. Smelling blood – shamelessly milking the situation – out came an intruding question to the Tory suit from Basil – now comfortably in the driving seat…

JR

Doesn't the government employ some company to get people back to work within the Department of Work and Pensions?

SUIT

Yes.

JR

Remind me who they are?

SUIT

(Grinning at me) *They are a company called ___*

                                   JR

(Butter wouldn't melt) *Oh I thought so* (Beat) *Am I right in saying that some of their former employees have recently been arrested and charged with something?*

                                  SUIT

                          I believe so, yes.

                                   JR

                       What are the charges?

                                  SUIT

                        Fraud, I believe.

I can't for the life of me remember what else was discussed on the program – canoeing in Wales for all I know. I was just floating on contentedness air with the fact that I'd got two opposing politicians to agree with me – and back me up – and the Conservative representative had even said a certain company's name on air.

I slept well that night.

Feedback

Via Email

Nice one Jonathan, stick at it. The only way to get these people to do anything is to embarrass them into it – Grayling and his mob do not like negative publicity.

Fireworks

Bonfire night 2013

Outside the winds were going some. See the garden furniture fly by. Inside it was warm, the atmosphere was what the Danish describe as *hygge* – cosy, there is no direct translation. The hour was mid-evening and guests clutched red wine and nattered pre- ignition of rockets, Catherine-wheels and sparklers. Some of the gathering were political professionals. One was an ex-prisoner.

As I chatted to one of the collective of the Westminster wagon – having admitted that I was the only representative of the latter clan paraphrased in the preceding paragraph he stopped me and Falstaff phrased – in a Brian Blessed blast – that he "had recently read in some official paperwork or other, of the most *ridiculous* episode where an intelligent prisoner had been stopped – in an *open prison* – from teaching some lag to read. Can you believe *that*?!"

I did my best to keep a straight face before uttering my reaction. That was me, I told him.

And I'm working my ass off to do something about it.

Proposed Mitigation

At around this time one of the bodies involved in prison reform got in touch with me. The caller was on a train. We had met before. It was a ghastly line and we kept being cut off. I think I was rung back nine times. Bloody tunnels.

"Jonathan. I know what you are trying to do – but what do you want from this? You've got Toe by Toe in all the prisons. Do you think what you're still doing is productive? Why don't you write to them (the education provider) and try and set up a meeting. Make peace."

In between tunnels MoJ meetings were transmitted – plus the fact that I had stood face to face with the head-honcho from the 'education provider' and told her first-hand what had occurred on their watch in an open – resettlement – prison. Further to that meeting emails had fired backwards and forwards and still no acknowledgment or responsibility had been taken.

"Yes, but what is this about? I know you are angry – and I support you. What happened was *wrong*, but why don't you try and get this sorted directly with them?"

The history of attempting that was again repeated. Explanation was passed that pre-publication they had been sent all relevant excerpts from the book but they had denied it was their man.

"What do you mean?"

I asked him if I could send a copy of the email which ludicrously indicated that they couldn't work out who their Head of Education was – before pointing out that illiteracy is rampant in our prisons and how dare this lot both bar purposeful activity in a pre-release prison and attempt to wriggle out of it with the flimsiest of excuses. He again tried to arbitrate an alternative strategy to my broadside of cannon shots aimed their way.

Again I repeated the question if I could send him a copy of their email. He relented. I sent it.

Five minutes later he called me back.

"I see what you mean. Now I understand. I don't blame you. Carry on Jonathan."

I thanked him and did so.

HENDLEY

Come on, Roger. We all know the score here, at least… most of us do. Your idea of this is to… start another front, to foul them up behind enemy lines. All right, that's fine. But once we get passed that, the mission is accomplished. Afterwards we may have some ideas of our own.

BARTLETT

You mean getting home? Back to your family?

HENDLEY

That's right.

BARTLETT

Good God, man. Do you really believe I haven't thought about that, too?

The Hundred Year Plan

Of late I do a lot of talking. Sorry about that. Sometimes it's even because I'm asked to. At a recent Howard League (for Penal Reform) function a gathering of students got the JR pitch. A fair number had contained and collated – loads of 'em. Inquisitive young eyes stared transfixed as my story came out. I spoke without notes for a good hour (poor things) and factored in my past, what I did to get myself into prison and what happened – or didn't – in jail. The optic feedback was eye-to-eye. The pupils' pupils not once wandered to the floor – like when politicians are being lectured on weather-worn clink chaos – folk who display a demeanour of not giving a toss. Electric was the atmosphere as they exquisitely expressed outrage at the debacle of the St Quentin Country Club known as HMP Hollesley Bay.

The audience had a generous share of very pretty girls within it. Every girl loves a pilot – I wish – and some were interested in how on earth an educated chap – an aviator at that – could have thrown it all away. The subject of aviation past being discussed – no skin off my nose, it helps illustrate what a clot I was and the contrast of what I discovered within prison of those less fortunate to have had my education – my breaks – my flying experience.

I kept the flight-path of aviation matters going. Flying has only recently celebrated its 100th birthday. Yet within that time we've put men on the moon, flown supersonic across the Atlantic and can travel to Europe on orange aeroplanes for less than a British Rail ticket from London to Brighton.

It's amazing really that something we all accept as par for the course has only been around a relatively short time yet we all just take it for granted. Especially young people.

Then it occurred to me. This audience had nodded their heads in moot agreement at my soapbox stance on rehabilitating prisoners via education rather than simply warehousing them – the soap opera floundering established formula, farcical, considering HRH has her name above the titles. There had been no 'we can't do that' reaction whatsoever like when one talks to tedious – elected – cack-handed politicians, incapable on the whole of admitting the total failure to motivate prisoners. I flagged the audience's overall reaction and revealed past conversations with suits and how refreshing it was to have common- sense prevail. If they could continue this train of thought – and pass it down to their offspring – maybe this country will, in a 100 years, via a change in philosophy, see a reduction in reoffending and the cerebral existing system finally scourged.

I hope so.

The Crown Prosecution Service (Part Two)

December 2013

Further audit fraud charge authorised in____case.

The CPS has today authorised a further charge against three women and two men in connection with alleged fraudulent activity at ___ (__), a social purpose company contracted by the Department of Work and Pensions (DWP) to deliver the '_____' employment and training scheme.

It is alleged that on or before 18 March 2011,_____ employees conspired to forge documentation in relation to services provided by _____, with the intention of convincing Department for Work and Pensions auditors that the documentation and claim for payment were genuine.

One of the women, already faces two existing charges relating to the alleged fraudulent activity at _____.

The five individuals are each charged with one count of conspiracy to make false instruments contrary to section 1(1A) of the Criminal Law Act 1977.

This decision to prosecute was taken in accordance with the Code for Crown Prosecutors.

We have determined that there is a realistic prospect of conviction and that a prosecution is in the public interest.

Rod Redemption (Part Ten)

The number tried again went straight to voicemail. This repeated over a number of days so a text went to the individual with whom I had last communicated on matters Rod.

A picture tells a thousand words…

Hello ▮▮▮ Jonathan Robinson here. Please can you give me a call. 12:06

Really busy, sorry . He is in ▮▮▮ prison. ▮▮▮ 14:09

Can you please call whenever you can.

RED

[narrating] I could see why some of the boys took him for snobby. He had a quiet way about him, a walk and a talk that just wasn't normal around here. He strolled, like a man in a park without a care or a worry in the world, like he had on an invisible coat that would shield him from this place. Yeah, I think it would be fair to say... I liked Andy from the start.

Mrs Robinson

Everyone asks me what happened. *Everyone*. I'll keep it short and sweet. An email arrived. I read it a few days after I got out of prison. In my local library.

The hangman could have done it better.

To hell with it, I have reproduced it below. I only hope by the time you read it, that its message has both faded in the picture and from my heart.

The latter is unlikely.

Nothing has changed, Mrs Robinson.

Nor will it.

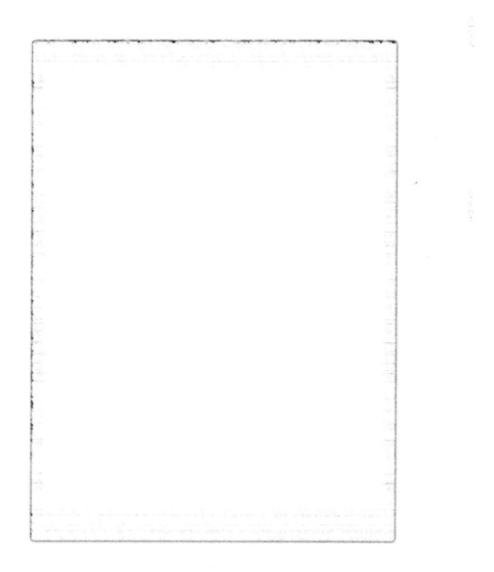

Prison Service Order

Order Number 2012-030

Earned Privileges Scheme (IEP)

Effective from 1 November 2013

This PSI sets out the revised operational framework for all prisons and Young Offender Institutions (YOIs) in delivering the Incentives and Earned Privileges Scheme (IEP), it follows a review of the IEP scheme, the outcome of which was announced by Ministers on 30 April 2013, and applies to all prisoners, male and female over 18.

Enhanced level:

To reach and remain on Enhanced status, prisoners must: Help other prisoners or prison staff e.g. Toe by Toe.

Guilty

Four former staff of scandal-hit dole-to-jobs firm admit swindling taxpayers

The Daily Mail

February 2014

Guilty Pleas yesterday followed an investigation into the troubled company which the government pays more than £200M each year. No date has been set for sentencing. Each faces up to 10 years in prison.

House of Commons

Wednesday 5 February 2014

The House met at half-past Eleven o'clock

PRAYERS

[Mr Speaker *in the Chair*]

Fiona Mactaggart (Slough) (Lab): When, on 22 February 2012, I asked the Prime Minister about fraud at ____ , a company working with jobseekers, he told me that he was waiting for the truth before he would act. This week's guilty pleas by ___ staff reveal a culture of fraud in that company. Is not the list of taxpayer-funded fraudsters getting too long? When is it going to stop?

The Prime Minister: The hon. Lady makes an important point. What we should do is investigate wrongdoing properly and make sure that cases are properly taken to court.

£17m Prison Education Contract Ended

The Guardian

August 13 2014

The welfare-to-work provider ___ has prematurely pulled out of a £17m contract to deliver education and training to prisoners in 12 London prisons on the grounds that it was unable to run the contract at a profit.

The decision was criticised by prison charities as likely to cause significant disruption for inmates.

Announcing that it would be terminating its contract, the company said delivering the Offender Learning and Skills Service (OLASS) had become "extremely challenging" in the past two years because of "a number of constraints" which had "a heavy impact on learner attendance, completion and achievements".

"We have concluded, in order to not continue to deliver the contract at a loss, to terminate our provision of [the contract] in London," it said. "This has been a very hard decision to make because ___ and its employees are passionate about the delivery of education services to offenders and believe education is critical to an offender's long-term rehabilitation."

The company, which was due to continue providing training until July 2016, employs 400 teaching and support staff within London prisons. ___ runs another teaching contract in prisons in the east of England which it has decided not to terminate.

___ did not specify the constraints it cited in its statement but prison charities said access to education in a number of prisons had been impeded by staff shortages which had hampered prisoners' ability to get to lessons. The company is paid according to the amount of training it provides.

The Skills Funding Agency said efforts had been made to find ways to allow ___ to continue delivering the contract but discussions had failed. The agency said it was working "to minimise disruption for learners in London prisons".

The start of ___'s prison education contract was complicated by a delay of several months as the company underwent an extra level of auditing, amid fraud allegations in its welfare-to-work contracts.

This is not the first time that ___ has prematurely terminated a prison education contract; the firm ended a similar contract providing education to eight prisons in Kent early in 2008, citing huge losses.

The decision to terminate service provision then was criticised by teaching unions, as evidence that outsourcing education contracts to private providers was not a reliable way to guarantee a good quality service.

Sadiq Khan, shadow secretary of state for justice, said: "This is a vote of no confidence by the private sector in the disastrous way the Government have allowed our prisons to descend into crisis. Providing good training and skills to offenders in prison is crucial in rehabilitation to stop them reoffending on release. Leaving prisoners to fester in their cells or on landings as a result of this shambles is no good for anyone."

House of Commons

Justice Committee Highlights

Oral evidence: Prisons: planning and policies, Tuesday 9 September 2014

Ordered by the House of Commons

Members present: Sir Alan Beith (Chair); Rehman Chishti; Jeremy Corbyn; John Cryer; Nick de Bois; Mr Elfyn Llwyd; and John McDonnell

Witnesses: Paula Harriott, Head of Programme, User Voice, Angela Levin, former Chair of HMP Wormwood Scrubs Independent Monitoring Board, Jonathan Robinson, former prisoner, and Deborah Russo, Prisoners' Advice Service, gave evidence.

Chair: Good morning and welcome. We are very grateful to you for coming in to help us with the work we are doing on prison planning and policies. We have with us this morning Angela Levin, formerly chair of the Wormwood Scrubs Independent Monitoring Board; Jonathan Robinson, who is a former prisoner and has written extensively; Paula Harriott, head of programme for User Voice; and Deborah Russo, joint managing solicitor for the Prisoners' Advice Service.

Jonathan Robinson: I want to be totally clear that I fully deserved a too-short prison sentence in 2011. I was sentenced to 15 months for theft. That was before the cuts. I fully deserved a prison sentence. What I saw going on — or not going on — in prison is part of the problem of the whole mess. When, quite justifiably, I was at the coal face — in the trenches — I found a prison officer asleep on duty on two occasions at HMP Bedford, which later transpired to be the prison with the highest suicide rate in England and Wales at the time. The stuff going on, or not going on — including, as I shall reveal later, in-house sabotage of rehabilitation — is the real root of the problem.

Jonathan Robinson: There are some very good prison officers. In my experience, there are also some awful ones. Prison officers in this country are trained for somewhere between six and eight weeks. In Norway, it is three years. In my experience, the majority of officers saw themselves as key handlers and not rehabilitators. That culture needs to change.

Chair: Mr Corbyn wants to come in on that.

Jeremy Corbyn: I thank Mr Robinson for what he has just said.

Jonathan Robinson: Jonathan.

Jeremy Corbyn: Welcome — thanks for coming along today.

Jonathan Robinson: It is a pleasure.

Jeremy Corbyn: Thank you to all of you. When you were there, were you able to have any serious conversations with prison officers about the nature of their work and how you and other inmates perceived them? Were they receptive to those kinds of discussions?

Jonathan Robinson: Yes. Believe you me, when you are allegedly intelligent and educated and you do something as daft as I did and end up in prison, the shock as to what is not going on is just life changing. I had many conversations with different officers in both of my prisons who were willing to engage. The passionate ones were as frustrated at the chaos and Monty Pythonesque stuff going on as a lot of the prisoners who wanted to engage and crack on. The officers with passion who expressed their issues talked about the frustration of the revolving door and seeing people leave the prison and come back. Throughout my whole prison journey, I saw missed opportunity after missed opportunity of fixing prisoners while they were in custody. It seems to me that a lot of recent reform has been focused on what prisoners call aftersales — the probation journey — rather than on what we could do with prisoners while we have them in custody. I totally echo Paula's earlier comments that, if you have a good ship's captain and there is good morale in a prison, that filters down to the staff and the prison. I go to a lot of prisons now — as a guest, I hasten to add — to give talks and to try to give encouragement, mostly to prisoners who are coming to the end of their journey. I tend to use a litmus test when I enter any prison, a bit like going into a new restaurant for the first time — I judge the atmosphere and what the interaction between the staff is like. At the beginning of the summer, I was at a prison where the governor knew all the prisoners' Christian names — and they were calling him by his Christian name. There was a buzz in that prison. My goodness, I was impressed. Everyone seems to think I am terribly negative about prisons. I am not — if I see something good, I will sing it from the rooftops. I really do agree with Paula — if you have a good ship's captain, you are halfway there. In my experience, staff with passion were as frustrated as I was about the mess. This was in 2011, so goodness knows how they are now.

Jonathan Robinson: The key issue, of course, is that 99% of prisoners will at some point be let out to rejoin society. I have been going on and on about trying to do more with them while we have them in custody. I have seen great stuff both in public sector prisons and in private prisons. In my experience and in the prisons where I have been to talk, neither one nor the other is ahead. It depends on the governor.

Chair: Mr Robinson?

Jonathan Robinson: Jonathan, please. You have just asked what is impeding resettlements. I would like to give you an example. I will start with a quote from the Prime Minister, who said that in prison "you'll...meet...people who can't read...These people need help...It's common sense." I am ashamed to say that before my fully justified prison sentence I had never heard of Toe By Toe or the Shannon Trust, which is a scheme, via phonetics, where literate prisoner A teaches illiterate prisoner B to read. I believe the figures for literacy in our prison population are that something like 75% have the reading level of an 11-year-old. In my closed-conditions prison, I was identified as being intelligent and literate and was trained to be a Toe By Toe mentor. Due to security issues before the cuts, I never got to tutor anyone in my closed-conditions prison, quite simply because there was no one on my wing who needed the help. I was told that there were plenty of prisoners on other wings who could do with help but, due to the then staff shortage, I was unable to tutor.

However, very early in my prison sentence I was moved to an open resettlement prison called HMP Hollesley Bay in Suffolk. On my first full day, I was identified as the only trained Toe By Toe mentor on site and asked whether I would be willing to teach two illiterate adult prisoners to read. Then and now, I was so ashamed of my behaviour and so eager to put something back in and to do something purposeful and constructive that I eagerly consented. I met the two prisoners who wanted me to teach them to read and set up appointments with them. On the afternoon of 1 September 2011, I was summoned to the office of the then head of education, a Mr _____ _____ from a company called ___, which was then being paid £7.6 million for its contract to provide prison education in the south-east. His exact words to me were, "Who told you to do Toe By Toe in this prison?" I told him, "The staff." He said, "Those people have no power in this prison. There will be no Toe By Toe in this prison. Scrub the appointments."

For the last three years, I have been trying to air the shooting down by in-house vested interests of a scheme championed by the Prime Minister, J. K. Rowling and Nick Hardwick. On my travels, I met the then justice director of ___, a Miss ___ _____. In writing, she indicated that the company was finding it difficult to identify which member of staff I was talking about. A number of e-mails flew backwards and forwards. Eventually, I sent Miss _____ a link to the ___ website, which names the head of education. I have not heard from the company since.

In meetings with the MOJ, after they asked me lots of questions about why prison does not work, they seemed primarily interested in the porn channels that were available at HMP Bedford. When I asked them what they were going to do about one of their service providers banning peer mentoring in an open resettlement prison, their response was, "We cannot comment on a specific incident."

Chair: Can I make two points to you? First, we have to give someone who is named the opportunity to answer criticisms you make of them.

Jonathan Robinson: Please do.

Chair: We will do so. Secondly, what do you think the motive of ___ might have been for excluding this form of mentoring and teaching from the prison?

Jonathan Robinson: As I said a moment ago, I have been independently working at prison reform and trying to reveal what is really not going on in prison. I have met an awful lot of important people, some of whom are very scared to admit what is really going on; they have said to me that they do not want to rock boats. Their opinion — and mine — is that the vested interests and all of the different agencies working in prison are wary of them doing the work, so they can show the results and, come renegotiation time, they can say, "Look at all the certificates we have gained for this. Look at all the people we have got off drugs," for example. They are stepping on one another's toes. In my experience, the vested interests within the system are part of the reason for the system per se shooting itself in the foot.

Worse, through all the work I have been doing on trying to air what is not going on, the Administration looks the other way or tries to ignore me. On 11 September last year, the MOJ very quietly announced that Toe By Toe was to become mandatory in all prisons. In prison, I met a great many prisoners who had done bad things — who deserved to be in prison and to be punished — but were full of talent. There is an army of enthusiastic prisoners wishing to engage who are shunned. I am just one tiny example. It is on the record that a month or so ago I had a meeting with the shadow Justice Minister. I said to him, "In an open resettlement prison, we had no walls — our boundaries were fields. If you have someone there who used to strip down engines, get him to teach the youngsters how to strip down engines."

One member of the panel talked about bounce-back engagement with staff. If you start giving young prisoners, in particular, encouragement and some sort of older brother relationship, whether it be with a prisoner who wishes to engage or with a good officer, you see their faces beam. Many of these people have never had a father figure. In my first prison, I had to teach youngsters how to make their beds.

Jonathan Robinson: From my experience in my work on prison reform, part of the problem is that the Administration — whichever side of the House it is — is very wary of the prison issue because they see it as potential trouble. When I was still a prisoner on licence, my services were utilised by ___ _____ MP, who wanted some feedback from me on prisons and who later promised me a reference so that I could return to employment. He made me that promise in writing and it was sent to the Civil Aviation Authority — I used to be a pilot. His exact words to me, referencing the Administration, were that "all politicians are terrified of the *Daily Mail* and the prison issue is an election loser."

Chair: This Committee is not terrified of any newspaper.

Jonathan Robinson: Incidentally, Mr _____'s promised reference was never forthcoming. The Civil Aviation Authority said in writing that that was spurious and grounded me.

Chair: I am afraid that that is another case where we will have to ask the person named whether they wish to respond.

Jonathan Robinson: I would welcome it.

Jonathan Robinson: I stress again that I was in prison for only 17 weeks, which in prison terms is a long weekend. I kept a prison diary, which everyone began to hear about. I remember a prisoner coming to me towards the end of my stay and saying, "Jonathan, will you use your influence to get some changes made?" I said, "I don't have any influence." He said, "No, no, no. Tell people what is going on."

Jonathan Robinson: When you sing this from the rooftops and see what really is not going on in prison, it is frustrating when the Administration just say, "Oh no, we are making prisons places of hard work and rehabilitation." It is about the inability of the system to say, "We have got one big problem." An Administration needs to say, "We all agree it is not working. Let's all hold our hands up and fix it." The Administration needs to lose its veil of saying, "No, it's fine, it's fine," which, I believe, is ultimately to keep certain newspapers happy because of this fear of elections. What they say is going on ain't going on. When you are there, you see the madness and the waste. If you then get to meet Mr Grayling to say, "This is what happens," you are told, "Oh, everyone is working hard." What is going on — or not going on — and what they say is going on are two different things.

Jeremy Corbyn: You have all expressed concerns about the way prisons are run. Jonathan, you also made a point about the lack of training of prison officers; indeed, the POA has made similar points to us. In a nutshell, could each of you give me your priorities for retraining or offering training to current prison officers and, of course, training of new prison officers?

Angela Levin: First, I would not have got rid of prison officers who had 20 or 25 years' experience. I would do anything to get them back. They are doing that. They spent £5 million on redundancy; they are now trying to get some of them back, which is a good sign. I would give them mental health training. They have about an hour to be taught how to deal with mental ill health.

Jeremy Corbyn: An hour?

Angela Levin: Yes. Incidentally, I would give the IMB mental health training, too, because it is very difficult to deal with prisoners who are very volatile and suddenly explode in your face. That is not done.

Deborah Russo: You cannot train someone in between six and eight weeks to become a prison officer. Maybe we should consider how it is done abroad.

Jeremy Corbyn: Which countries would you look at?

Deborah Russo: Scandinavia.

Jeremy Corbyn: We visited Norwegian prisons. I was impressed with them.

Jonathan Robinson: And compare the reoffending.

Jeremy Corbyn: It is very low.

Paula Harriott: I would concur.

Jonathan Robinson: To answer your question, yesterday I was outside HMP Bedford for an interview. They have a notice on the wall advertising prison officer vacancies. One of the strap-lines was "No academic qualifications required."

Chair: This Committee has in the past lamented the shortness of prison officer training here by comparison with almost every other developed country. I thank the four of you for the help you have given this morning. We appreciate it very much indeed.

To plug… or not

"*Man…*" winced Mario Andretti, the 1978 F1 © World Champion, when reminiscing about the sublime Colin Chapman penned title clinching Lotus 79; "that car went round corners like it was painted to the road… like it was on *rails…*"

The © appears in the above sentence because I don't want Bernie Ecclestone on my back for copyright infringement – despite giving the sport I love a plug.

More of plugs later.

Dramatis personæ who appear further into these words carry no warrant worthy of jitterbugs from this alleged author, so rest assured the following is a health-and-safety and whitewash free zone. For upcoming is/are the bare facts on the latest shenanigans concerning this idiot and prison reform.

Prison. A place where drugs are a given commodity. Stored about vendors where the sun doesn't shine. Drugs that make you high – to numb the time. Or drugs that make you look like Arnold Schwarzenegger – yet stored within the purveyor's rear end.

An arse about face way of beefing up then.

Andretti again (bear with me)… and rails… railroads…

Please be assured that after just shy of three years, I have tried my utmost to address various oddities witnessed in jail via gentle negotiation. Apart from the MoJ very quietly announcing in September of 2013 that Toe by Toe was to become mandatory in all prisons, my clameur de haro has been met with a deaf ear cold shoulder combo that marches in time. No one in power has come anywhere close to getting to the bottom of what was really going down – on the rehabilitation front – and why – as it bottomed-out during my tenure as a guest of HRH after I had sent myself up the river and then attempted to air-lift in a scheme the system had earmarked and trained me to tutor after being parachuted into an open resettlement prison, the soft landing refused. Thus when the Justice Select Committee approached me to reveal all – on Westminster's doorstep – it was the MoJ/HMPS management's previous toe-curling silence that railroaded me to consent to turning up at the House of Commons early-doors on September 9th 2014, determined to make the fur fly – and play merry hell with the Praetorian Guard who manage our jail system reference the Kamikaze in-house, in-prison shooting down of a reading plan (*raved* about by the Prime Minister) three years post factum. Terrifyingly, I have learnt, this raw deal for rehabilitation by no means of isolated incidence, frighteningly my experience of purposeful activity being stymied is the tip of the iceberg. For all serving prisoners, those wishing to be productive, of which there are, believe it or not; plenty, I have continued to be a voice crying in the wilderness and complete pain in the neck to get matters various brought to a conclusion.

Before the appointed day, the world and his wife (within political circles) were consulted on how best to play this. The primary counsel sought was centred on the fact that witnesses appearing are effectively given parliamentary privilege – safe conduct from any court, regardless of what one says – and I was uncertain whether I should *hint* at who/what/where/why or… name and shame…

Everyone – and I mean *everyone*, including folk who appear on the front of newspapers, told me – firmly – to go with plan B… with a hammer.

Having been in it and on it, I was now under it.

Therefore the plan for my big game baptism at Westminster was to go in at more than a fair bat – to truly bandy words. Someone had to make a song and dance about our failing prison system whose management keep declaring that all is tickety-boo. Yeah – and Barratt's built Stonehenge. A bitter pill for them to swallow – but the hot air PR bilge water they sprout is bunkum, woefully wide of the mark. Their total refusal to cry peccavi on the comic-strip that is rehabilitation, effectively washing their hands of the debacle, galvanised me to lay on the table the naked truth. The hard sell on the hocus-pocus it had to be. Even if it caused heebie-jeebies. Total sink or swim – but smoke them out with a taste of the rope's end, for faint heart never won fair lady.

Adytum walking through the House of Commons as an ex-prisoner – as one does – having arrived at an ungodly hour,

I don't mind admitting I was nervous. The interior of Parliament; all those paintings, sculptures and Powell and Pressburger dramatic light – oh the colours – pouring through cinema screen sized windows that threw narrow-eyed suspicious stage-fright at me. Here I was. Get it right Robinson. Tell them what's really happening in prison. And stop shaking. But it's going out on the telly… Shut up – just get on with it.

Like I said; nervous.

Before blast-off Jonathan Aitken instructed me to "speak for England". So no pressure then. Indubitably thinking once more unto the breech, in I went.

I think and hope I got the key points over. I hit the ground running as my hat was hurled into the ring. The wasted, missed opportunity of rehabilitation in prison, witnessed first-hand in the field of fire, resulting in many inmates falling by the wayside because the artillery is shooting blanks. As I let my hair down on cold steel facts, none of the Committee seemed surprised, indeed feedback was good. Subtle – but satisfying.

I noticed the odd eyebrow being cocked as I broached the damp squib cack-handed so called fifth-wheel rehabilitation seen taking place in our jails. When the howler of the hors de combat of Toe by Toe – in an open resettlement prison – was relayed, I clocked two of them shaking their heads.

I talked a lot about prisoners marking time rather than making time which in turn fuels the revolving door – how the non-newspaper reading staff, or those asleep on duty – had expressed their frustration to me to seeing folk leave prison only to horrifically boomerang back. The gathered politicians and the Committee's Chairman – Sir Alan – sat ashen faced.

Incidentally, I had to be firm with myself not to make any *Apprentice* 'Sir Alan' jokes – for sitting in front of this lot was just like that show on the box.

It's a small world. I left the House of Commons – the wheels within wheels – where it's at – on the mark of 1115 and at 1130 the professionals sat – and the following happened:

House of Commons

Tuesday 9 September 2014

The House met at half-past Eleven o'clock

PRAYERS

[Mr Speaker *in the Chair*]

Oral Answers to Questions

JUSTICE

The Lord Chancellor and Secretary of State for Justice (Chris Grayling): "*I pay tribute to all the volunteers in the toe by toe programme, and to all the prisoners who can read and devote time to helping those who cannot. It is important that we take advantage of all the resources available to us to try to tackle the problem of a lack of literacy in our prisons.*"

Are you thinking what I'm thinking? Less than thirty minutes after my oral evidence and Mr Grayling sings praises for Toe by Toe in the House of Commons. Coincidence? It certainly looked all a bit last minute – he appeared to have knotted his tie in the dark. Gok Wan would have a *fit*.

Aitken again. A full de-brief post event. He didn't half like my plea for good governors. He spoke of being somewhere during his innings for HRH where the governor was more than asleep at the wheel. Some new fella was wheeled in – ironically called Robinson he chuckled – who noticed a somewhat submerged atmosphere and promptly got the entire ship's company to repaint some of the more dilapidated buildings. Aitken concluded that with the activity – the place was truly lifted to new heights…

That evening there was some press about the hearing. The education provider announced they were "disappointed" by my evidence. The same emotion was transmuted through social media. Disappointed at my version of what took place, or disappointed that the truth be declared so publically, in such historic surroundings?

Then the next day – things got interesting. For through social media the following attempt to eclipse the facts and dowse the fire popped up…

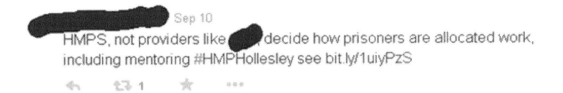

Fiddle-de-dee. That old "it wasn't us" chestnut again… all fine and dandy… but I need you to come back in time with me… Toe by Toe was barred in an open prison on the afternoon of September 1st, 2011. After the Head of Education had firmly declared "*The person who told you to do Toe by Toe has no power in this prison. There will be no Toe by Toe in this prison. Scrub the appointments*" I immediately queried his odd strategy – also asking what I could do about his rather at-odds decision. He definitively ordered me to return to the in-house agency who were responsible for who-did-what (prisoner wise) at HMP Hollesley Bay. This I did and the individual responsible for in-prison employment said "red tape is all over the place" and told me "to leave it with him".

I did so. For more than a week. A 1/10th of my time at the Bay.

At 1015 on Monday, September 12th, 2011 I wrote to the giver of jobs – or to quote the social media used by the education provider in the vernacular they have utilised, the HMPS allocator of work, and asked him if he had any news on a shift back to common sense from the Head of Education. I was desperate to do something purposeful and not just tread-water in prison.

On Tuesday, September 13th, 2011 – or in plain English, the next day, I saw and spoke with the addressee of my letter – this man responsible for all employment – who confirmed that he was in receipt of it and that it was "now on the Head of Education's desk."

Thus, the in-house agency for employment was doing its best to get me up and running at Toe by Toe. Per contra, it was not the employment allocator – but the Head of Education that was the spanner in the works.

On the following day, Wednesday, September 14th, 2011, at 0845 I again pleaded with the employment boss to try and make the Head of Education change his mind. I repeated my frustration of being unable to help people who *wanted to learn to read*. I sensed his annoyance too. He hinted that there would be stern words from him soon towards the Head of Education. He closed with "It was a shame" that I was not going to be in the prison for longer (I only had about nine more weeks to go) to allow more time to "sort this out." I promised him that I'd lob a brick through a jeweller's window so they could bring me back.

I could go on…

Back to the Education provider and social media. As well as implying that it was the jobs allocator responsible for Toe by Toe not happening – this gem appeared too:

Sep 10

…HMPS teams highly expert in making appropriate judgements to ensure a safe regime and effective risk management.

Which I assume was a dig at me by implying I was not fit to tutor Toe by Toe, which the *system* had trained me to do. Me – someone who had for 20 years or so tutored folk the trivial act of flying helicopters. Oh – and if I was of risk – why did I end up emptying waste paper baskets (10 minutes a day – exhausting stuff) in Healthcare… where all the drugs were… where on Monday, October 24th, 2011, (0720) I found two TV sized boxes full of drugs… A high risk prisoner would no doubt, have gone into business and opened up shop.

I handed them in.

Seems to me the education provider needs to try a different tack – if they wish to continue shirking from the responsibility… Prison taught me to have a yen for fair play. From my worm's eye view I sense a sham. Their ongoing blind spot refusal to face reality beats Banagher – a fly in the face of everything prison is supposed to do, after they forced, via a putsch, a proven to reduce reoffending reading scheme to take an early bath. Mega quantities of shekels are flying around within the pantomime identikit of prison education. Cui bono? There's the rub. That computer room – for prison education – at Hollesley Bay – which sat *empty* still haunts me. You'd see more activity at the *Playboy Magazine* storage department in Alan Carr's residence.

Two days later I was back at the House of Commons – I might apply for a season ticket – for a pre Justice Committee arranged meeting with one Simon Hughes MP – a real live Justice Minister. He and I had been on the BBC a month or so earlier and a tête-à-tête seemed logical. Perhaps this would shed new light…

Normally – from past experience – meetings with Suits necessitates others being on site – the odd assistant here, an advisor there, but as I waited in that vast atrium again, a familiar face hovered too. A lady. I had spotted her at the Justice Committee hearing (*frantically* taking notes – in shorthand) and asked her if she was the stenographer or a journalist? "No, I'm from the MoJ." (Whoops!) Another individual loitered too – who identified himself from the Skills and Funding agency – the sugar daddy that pays for prison education. They were both pleasant and polite – but boy did I get the impression that I was not exactly the toast of the town for having recently sung that the king has no clothes on – and perhaps more vitally, who had ripped the garments off.

Down we were escorted. And I mean down to the *depths*. As I contemplated being *Prisoner of Zenda* taken to some deep dungeon in the foundations of Parliament instead of trial by minister, I was more than looking over my shoulder for a Guy Fawkes trail for escape in the opposite direction.

A cell it wasn't that we arrived at, but the Minister's office. He was welcoming. We all sat down. MoJ Lady kept saying "yes Minister" to him which nearly gave me the giggles. I addressed him as Sir so as not to self-implode in fits of laughter. He acknowledged the drum-beating from my direction on prison reform and – eyebrows northbound – referred to my locked horns appearance at the Justice Committee – all the world and his wife in CJS circles now know what happened. He, whilst resolved to what had occurred, did not seem thrilled. I got the distinct impression that I had well and truly left an apple-pie bed in the apple of discord.

It was agreed that I rattle off my previously prepared list (never go to the House of Commons without a list). This I did. All the usual stuff. I won't itemise it – if you're reading this, you already know. The Full Monty on the Ealing Comedy ghost train that is our HMPS's failure flooded out. Some of the hot potatoes I will reveal that were discussed include the induction paperwork from HMP Bedford – the system's kick-off on the rehabilitation process – *stuffed* with spelling mistakes.

The Minister's response: "There is no excuse for this". I gave him a copy of the three line email received from Hollesley Bay's MP which ended with "I have nothing to add" when I had been house-to-house, from Dan to Beersheba, *desperate* to reveal the lowlife slow-handclap well-and-truly-missed-the-bus middle ages rehabilitation free-fall going on in her local open prison – leaving no stone unturned. The Minister looked plain uncomfortable scrutinising it. I questioned why the (then) Prisons Minister had never replied to a letter of mine reference Hollesley Bay/Toe by Toe events. I sang like a canary about the MP who had used my services – whilst I was an on-licence prisoner – for *his* prison book – *assuring* me – in *writing* – a reference so I could return to employment. That reference never came, forcing the Civil Aviation Authority (400 years ago I used to be a pilot) to declare the silence was spurious and grounded me.

When I got to the topic of the nadir – the in house sabotage of rehabilitation, MoJ lady was very quick to say things Toe by Toe were now "much better". This I totally consented to – I have seen it with my own eyes in many of the prisons I give talks at.

However – this did not remedy my order of interest. The cardinal point of what happened on September 1st, 2011, the banning of a scheme ("here's one thing that we *know* that works in prison" – Nick Hardwick, Chief Inspector of prisons) by the education provider's little Corporal. In front of the Minister I said the following:

Is anyone here – for one second – in any way shape or form, arguing my version of events reference the barring of Toe by Toe in an open resettlement prison?

She – lips thinned – hatchet faced – in *front* of the Minister slowly shook her head.

Lo and behold, at *last*, finally; a horse of a different colour. No contest; *nolo contendere*, now you're talking... But, if those at the helm were now admitting it – why in god's name can't the fake tan education provider? Their social media declaration that job allocation is not their bag – and inability to address the key issue and decree an *amende honorable* – whilst Ministry folk are declaring no argument, is just another stunning example of the lack of dot to dot synchronicity within the system. Heath Robinson, eat your heart out – and at the same time; fill your boots. A refusal to acknowledge the corn; that we have a hard boiled prison system well adrift and – *Glory Hallelujah* – my log now beyond question.

Talk about relief.

With the system now well and truly over a barrel, I voiced that with all the past bats in the belfry doolally denials, would the Ministry now act? Some individuals need to be hung higher than Gilderoy's kite. The Minister explained that due to Parliamentary etiquette he had to hold off until the Justice Committee published its findings.

As I write, I wait with baited breath.

Afterwards the Skills Funding Agency representative told me that he had found no evidence of a scorched earth policy at the central HQ of the education provider – and he was fairly sure the banning of Toe by Toe was for other reasons. Perhaps the man at the Bay just didn't like me? If it's any conciliation, I wasn't too fond of myself at the time – however, I was trying to do *right*.

This collection of words set out with matters plug. Later that evening, having been all week on what felt like the receiving end of trial by bar, this individual became a prisoner at the bar and I sat outside a local watering hole sipping a beer desperately trying to shake things prison from my mind. Difficult with nearly three years slogging away. Even harder when I started to eavesdrop on a conversation between two young men sitting at a nearby table...

One had just got out of prison.

The other was on his way there the next day. It's called HMP recycling.

The topic was where best to hide the phone.

The advice was simple:

"Plug it"

The receiver of this eye-watering advice didn't look too thrilled with this suggestion – and shifted uncomfortably in his chair.

I will leave it to you dear reader to use your imagination as to where the phone was headed.

Mario Andretti would have winced again.

Epilogue

RED

Rehabilitation? Well now, let me see... No, I don't have any idea what that means... To me it's just a made up word so young fellows like yourself can wear a suit, a tie and have a job.

Rehabilitation? It's just a bullshit word.

Printed in Great Britain
by Amazon